M000084545

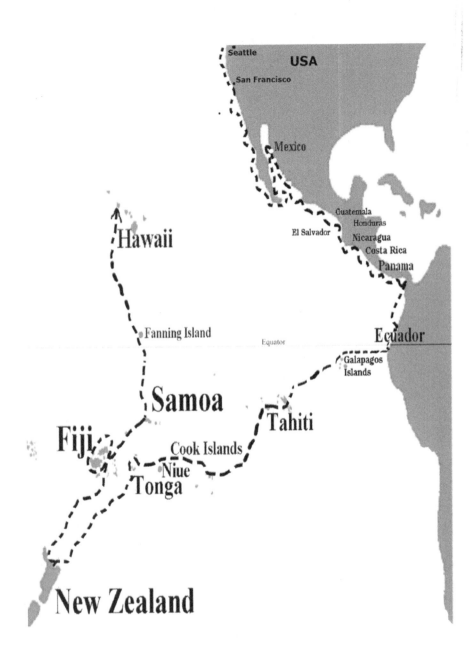

Seattle

USA

San Francisco

Mexico

Guatemala
Honduras
El Salvador
Nicaragua
Costa Rica
Panama

Hawaii

Fanning Island

Equator

Ecuador

Galapagos
Islands

Samoa

Tahiti

Fiji

Cook Islands

Niue

Tonga

New Zealand

ONE MAN'S DREAM
ONE WOMAN'S REALITY

A six year sailing adventure

SHARON REED-HENDRICKS

with Steve Hendricks

Copyright © 2013 Sharon Reed-Hendricks

All rights reserved.

ISBN-10:0962973521
ISBN-13:9780962973529

ALSO BY SHARON REED-HENDRICKS:

FROM WHERE EAGLES SOAR

SHARON SHARES HER HEART

TO OUR TWELVE GRANDCHILDREN

Cody

Nick

Miranda

David

Aaron

Christiaan

Bailey

Maliyah

Hunter

Keira

Mattea

Finn

Dream and make it your reality

CONTENTS

ACKNOWLEDGMENTS

As with many books, this one would never have been born without the help of many who never gave up on me when I felt like giving up on myself. In Hawaii, "Mahalo" means "Thank You." Mahalo to Debbie Graves who took my newsletters and somehow put them on a thumb drive, saving me hours of re-typing. Mahalo to Linda Staton and Anna Warlick our editors, for endless hours of help. Mahalo to Judy McCluskey and Anne Fisher who gently pushed me to get the book done. To my daughters Tracy and Tiffany who helped with technical parts as they have more computer knowledge than their mother. To my daughter Michelle for all her encouragement. To my walking partners, Marge, Chris and Corinne for listening to my frustrations as we walked the lagoons. I'm sure they wondered if this book would ever get finished. To all my neighbors at Ko Olina Marina for their love and support. Mahalo to my long-distance friends, Pat Conger and Carolann Friges who listened for hours as I talked about the book. And to all the ladies in my yoga class and lunch group for your friendship and love. A special mahalo to Dr. Dean Nelson my coach, for all his insight and help when I was stuck. And to Steve, my husband and best friend, for never giving up on us. Mahalo to everyone who has ever touched my life or ever will—you are the reason I live and thrive on this planet.
Mahalo Nui Loa

FORWARD

The Dream and the Reality

As I start to write, I realize it has taken me over five years to sit down and do this. I had many excuses; too busy, no time, no money, no one to help. I know now I was avoiding it. I am out of excuses, so it is time. This is the reality. The dream is gone and I am awake and facing reality.

To write about the dream that we lived is almost painful. There were good days and bad days, but most of it was good. It feels as if someone has died. In a way someone has. The dream is gone now and only lives in my mind and in the journals I kept of everyday I lived the dream. And now it lives again in the pages I write about the journey we took, the dream we lived and the reality of it all.

In life we all have dreams; dreams of having something, building something, going somewhere, doing something. With every dream there is a price to pay—the reality.

If you're dreaming of becoming a doctor or dentist or lawyer, then you pay the price of many years of study. If you dream of that big home, then you pay the price of keeping up the payments, the yard and the responsibility that goes with having a big house. You get the drift. There's a price to pay for everything.

Steve is the dreamer and I'm the realist. Steve's dream was to have a sailboat and sail it all over the world. It soon became my dream but I knew there was a price to pay. We were gone for six years. Although we flew back home twice in those six years, we missed out on spending time with family and friends and the births of several grandchildren. We also missed out on six years of building our retirement accounts, as we were not working those years. But I knew the price before we left and looking back I wouldn't trade those six years for the world. Yet I guess I did trade them and I got the world. And the world changed me.

I am not the same person that left Seattle that sunny August day in 1999. I've learned so much about the world and myself. I learned I don't need all that "stuff" anymore. Less is really more. I learned to relax and enjoy nature. I know now that we are all the same inside no matter what color our skin or what language we speak. Music and love are the international language. And people everywhere are wonderful if you really take the time to get to know them.

Sharon Reed-Hendricks
Ko Olina, Hawaii

The Storm

Sharon Reed-Hendricks

The night was dark - no moon, no stars
The seas were building fast
The wind she howled - and she was loud
How long would this storm last?

The seas were huge - our boat so small
And all around we tossed
I could not see - rain pelted me
I worried we'd be lost

The wind raged on - the seas roared back
Their fight went on for days
I could not eat - stand on my feet
For I was in a haze

Below the cabin all a mess
Things tossed and broke and wet
The sails were torn and I was worn
This storm I wouldn't forget

And then the fight was over
As quick as it begun
The seas subside - the wind she died
And no one really won

I looked out through the sunlight
At turquoise sea so grand
Green hills so bright - and sand so white
And there before me – Land!

VIII

1   The Storm

Sharon

I sit below at the chart table, plotting our course when I hear that sound again. It sounds just like a huge train bearing down on us. I hold onto the chart table with both hands and wait as every two to three minutes it happens. Then it hits us and for a few seconds I am airborne. When it's over, my tears fall to the chart and I whisper, "Please God don't let us die."

From Steve's Log:

August 14th, 1999.   All day the winds have been building. The forecast is for 20 to 25 knots, but we already have 20 knots and gusting to thirty with twelve foot seas. We are south of Cape Mendocino about a hundred miles north of San Francisco, near Fort Bragg, California. We're too far out to make it to safety. We didn't rig our storm sails (a decision we would later regret) because the forecast was for improving conditions. I knew we were in trouble when Tommy, a seasoned sailor, said these steep seas were as bad as anything he'd ever seen, even in the Southern Ocean.

By evening, we can no longer sail our course. We have to run down wind to keep the waves from rolling us. As it gets dark the wind increases its fury to 30 knots with gusts to forty. This is not fun. We are all scared but afraid to say so. Sharon calls the Coast Guard to get a weather update, but they say, "The forecast is still only 20 to 25 knots moderating at midnight." She tells them it's already more than that out here. She asks the guardsman if he will keep in radio contact until we are safely through this. He says they do not do that, but she gets the officer in charge and he agrees to the hourly check to make sure we are okay.

It is now far too rough and dangerous to send anyone on deck to rig the storm sails, so we roll up all but five feet of our roller jib

1

(the main is already down) to further reduce the boat speed, but we are still hitting 10 knots coming down some of these big waves. Steering is so strenuous and exhausting that Tommy and I are trading off every thirty minutes. At about 9:00 p.m. we hear a terrifying loud crack. The upper rudder shaft housing has broken. From now on we will have to be extremely careful not to pull too hard on the tiller or we may cause more damage. During this time we were tethered to the boat with lifelines to keep from falling overboard. By midnight the wind is a steady 40 knots and gusting to fifty and the seas are huge—about twenty-five feet high and steep. The waves look like a two story building coming at us in full force. As they wash under us, they lift our stern first and then the whole boat goes up, then over the top of the wave we go and back down the trough again. Each time the wind slows down a little, we think it's over, but it just comes roaring back stronger than ever.

Both Tommy and I are amazed at how well Sharon is holding up through all this. She is keeping hot coffee and food coming, as well as doing all the radio calls and keeping track of our position on the chart and GPS. She is also watching the radar for other ships in the area.

At 2:00 a.m. the wind is howling louder than ever. The noise is terrifying. Each wave sounds like a freight train coming at us in the dark, and the wooden parts of the boat are groaning and creaking loudly. We are beginning to hit cross-waves at a different angle from the wind waves. When we hit one of these, it sends ten to twenty gallons of cold water into the cockpit. If the helmsman doesn't duck, it goes right down his neck. Furthermore, tops of some of the waves are blowing off now hitting us like hard rain. We are all very exhausted and numb to the chaos going on around us. Finally at about 4:30 a.m. the wind slacks off to 25 knots. This feels like no wind at all compared to what we have just been through. (The force of the wind quadruples when the wind doubles, so 40 knots is like four times stronger than 20 knots.)

Sharon
As my head was nodding at the chart table, I was thinking, "How

2

the hell did I get here and why did I ever decide to take this journey?" I started thinking back over the past several years and remembering just how I fell in love with sailing and with Steve.

Steve and I met when we were both in our forties, both been married before and both had children. I had four, three girls and one boy. Steve had two daughters. My oldest daughter had a baby boy so that made me a grandmother and Steve a grandfather when we married almost three years later. Actually, we met at a Backcountry Horseman convention (we both had horses at the time) where I was asked to write and recite an inspirational poem. I also sold copies of my self-published poetry book at the event. Steve bought a copy of my book; as I autographed the front page I looked up at his familiar face and asked the old line, "Don't I know you from somewhere?" He replied "Maple Valley." it was the town where I lived and the one where he used to live. And then he said, "The Hardware Store" (Steve is a man of few words, unlike me). Then I remembered, I had thought he was the janitor as he always had a broom in his hand and a million keys dangling from his belt. I later learned that he was the owner. He asked me about my promotional advertising company and I gave him a business card and told him a little about what I did. He started calling me and ordering items on a regular basis. I would call him to let him know his item was in (he ordered a lot of business cards) and to ask when I should ship them. Amazingly he was always going to be down in my area the week his order arrived and could we meet for coffee, or lunch or breakfast and I could deliver the order then. We met over many cups of coffee and many lunches. Steve went through more business cards than anyone I knew. He became a mentor of mine as he helped me with several business ideas. We became good friends and I looked forward to our meetings.

At Steve's suggestion, we always seemed to meet at a location on the water. I loved the water so that was just fine with me. I loved watching the boats sail by. One day I mentioned to Steve that I would like to learn to sail and he said he sailed and would love to teach me. That sounded too much like a date and I didn't want to date anyone for a while, as I had been in a bad marriage and was

3

only a few years into recovery from alcohol. I went home that night and wrote Steve a letter explaining that I didn't want to get involved with anyone right now and explained why. He wrote back that he didn't want to get involved either. That took a big load off my mind. Now I could relax. We wouldn't get involved.

At that time I was taking flying lessons and was eager to share my excitement with Steve. He told me that he understood the excitement as he had his pilot's license. Was there anything this guy couldn't do? He was really becoming a good friend so I asked him to teach me to sail.

Steve taught me to sail and I fell in love with sailing and with Steve. So I guess our entire life together has been on or around the water. I put flying on the back burner and concentrated on sailing.

Neither of us had much money when we met, so the idea of owning a sailboat and taking off to sail the world seemed like a crazy dream. Because I owned my own company I was very independent. The thought of just being on a sailboat the size of a walk-in closet, with a man, let alone living on a sailboat that size, with a man, made my blood run cold. In fact I told Steve, "I would *never* live on a boat nor would I *ever* sell my business and sail around the world. And did he understand that?" And he said, yes, he did understand. So that took care of that. A few months later we were looking at sailboats to buy.

We had $5,000 to our name, and even in 1993 that didn't buy very much. But we were in love and had a dream. When two people work together on the same dream, it happens twice as fast. So it wasn't long when one day we were walking the docks at the Everett marina in Washington and there she was. The old Buchan sailboat, sort of derelict looking, but in our price range sailboat. She was 37 feet long and had a narrow beam of less than ten feet. She needed a new interior and those orange countertops were a big concern of mine. Steve assured me we could change the interior and the countertops; it was the hull and the structure of the boat that mattered. We needed to do a haul-out and look at the bottom. I knew very little about boats at that time; as long as I could change those countertops and decorate the place I would be okay. Did I mention she also had no refrigerator, no hot water, no real cooking stove, and just a big old- fashion heating stove? This is the Northwest you know. The head (bathroom) was kind of, well not very nice. The bed did not look very comfortable with a one-inch foam cushion similar to those in the main salon. Basically, she was a mess. But we had a vision and we were going to make her beautiful. I still had no intention of living on the boat let alone sailing it all over the world, but the idea was entering my mind. We did a haul-out, negotiated a price ($25,000) and with $5000 down and monthly payments for a few years, we had us a sailboat. We had already picked out a name so during our next haul-out we christened her S/V (sailing vessel) *Poet's Place*, since I'm a poet.

The slip fees (rent) at the marina were very cheap at that time, which enabled us to double up on our boat payments while working on the boat. Every weekend we spent at the boat, working, fixing, varnishing and dreaming. Somewhere in there, we found time to get married at our little house on the lake where we were spending less and less time.

Spending so much time at the marina on the boat, you get to meet a variety of characters who also own boats. Some of them lived on their boats and some have sailed all over the world and have fascinating stories to tell. Being the type of person that I am, with a big imagination, I was soon picturing myself sailing the islands of the South Pacific in my bikini, eating papaya and swimming with the dolphins. This image made me work even faster and harder and put a crazy idea into my head. I announced to Steve one day that maybe I should sell my business and we should sell everything and move onto the boat. This way we could sail the world sooner rather than later when we are too old. This of course, was what Steve had been waiting for (he has more patience than I). So there we were, at the tender age of forty eight, with no money to speak of and a derelict boat getting ready to sail around the world.

I sold my business, which was very emotional, as I had built this promotional advertising company after my divorce, from nothing into the success that it had become. It was a part of me. Although I knew I was helping to finance a dream, and it was my idea and my decision, it was still very difficult. I sold it to a girl who had the same type of business; the arrangement we worked out was that she would make monthly payments based on sales from my clients, for two years. This arrangement worked out quite well and made me feel like I was contributing each month to our dream. Steve continued to work his full time job as the manager of a feed and farm store located about twelve miles from the boat.

Then we had the garage sale. Everything had to go. The kids came and took what they wanted and when they said they had enough we sold the rest. I didn't realize we had so much stuff. I had a melt-down when someone wanted to buy the old chest of drawers with shelves that came from my old house. As I was helping to move this chest, I noticed the little hole my son had made to thread his radio cord through to plug into the wall. At that exact moment, my son arrived and hollered into the room, "Mom are you home?" All the memories of all those years came flooding back in the form of tears. I just broke down and cried. Later that evening Steve and I sat in our empty house and looked out the window at the sunset over the lake. I cried my eyes out and asked, "Steve, why are we doing this. Why are we leaving this beautiful place?" Steve's answer was, "So we can see sunsets all over the world." That must have been the right answer, because I dried my tears and said okay.

The only item left in the house was the old trunk that I was saving to bring to my oldest daughter. I sat down and wrote this poem after I opened the trunk.

The Trunk

Sharon Reed-Hendricks

Today I opened up the trunk
And filtered through my tears
I relived every memory
Of the past 30 years

6

It's time for me to move on now
The kids are grown and gone
It's time to give away or sell
The things I've had so long

I sold and threw away a lot
But just put off till last
The trunk with all the memories
My hold onto the past

The baby books and handmade cards
And little outfits too
I guess I just couldn't part with them
And the memories of you

And then I came across the card
A small handprint inside
A poem about your fingerprints
And then I really cried

I thought of you - all grown up now
My grandson's hands that size
And through the tears of memories
I began to realize

In order to grow - I must let go
And time moves on with ease
The trunk is yours; I'll pass it on
But I'll keep the memories

We didn't have a house to sell as we were renting with the option to buy. We opted not to buy at this time and since we had no more furniture and very few possessions, we packed our cars and moved on the boat. Something I said I would never do. I must have been crazy at the time, but somehow I didn't mind living without all those conveniences of a house because I saw the dream and it was

7

worth it. Steve was working full time and I was now unemployed after selling my business a few months earlier. We spent every weekend working on the boat and I worked almost every day, sanding, varnishing, sewing and planning.

Steve said it would take about two years to get the boat finished. I soon learned that when I asked how long a project would take or how much something would cost, I would just double the time and the price and that figure would be more accurate. I also saved myself some disappointment. The boat took five years to finish.

At about year three, we had to do a haul-out to rebuild the rudder, paint the bottom, and re-paint the topsides and the decks. We took a boat painting class to learn how to paint the boat. Haul-out is when they pull your boat out of the water with a lift and set the boat on the ground (thus the name dry dock). To get into the boat, you have to climb a twelve-foot ladder. You cannot flush your toilet as there is no salt water to flush with, so you climb down the ladder to use the marina bathroom or at night you use the bucket and chuck it method. Nobody really likes living on the boat while you're in haul-out, but unless you're rich and can afford a hotel room this is the preferred method. It also allows you to start work first thing in the morning and work till dark with one partner (guess who) taking a break to cook a meal. Steve said we would be in haul-out hotel for about five weeks. We were there for four months and I really thought we would never float again.

Steve is very handy and can build or fix anything, which comes in handy when sailing offshore. He rebuilt everything on the boat (with my help). He rebuilt the anchor windless and bow rollers (holds the two main anchors) and the arch to hold our solar panels while taking a welding class at the local college. He rebuilt a water maker that we bought second hand. He installed the new generator for our refrigerator and put in a new stove and oven. He rewired our electrical system, rebuilt our companion way (entry to the cabin below) and added new storage boxes in the cockpit. He redid the plumbing and rebuilt the steps into our main salon having each step open for storage. We added lights and radios for single side-band and ham radio. We designed and built a three-part nested din-ghy. We took a ham radio class and both became ham radio opera-tors. For me, the ham radio became my lifeline while crossing the ocean.

In the mean time I was busy sewing cushions and curtains, awning and covers. I also started writing articles for the sailing magazines about getting a boat ready for cruising. I talked with everyone in our marina and toured every boat that I could and came back with new ideas and projects for Steve to work on. I also started to make a list for our medical kit and provisioning for our food storage. We made a great team.

We were completely self-sufficient on that boat. In the back portside berth, Steve carried all his tools and extra parts for the boat. On the back starboard side, I carried all our food supplies. We had enough food to last six months and enough tools to build an-other boat.

Looking back over those five years, I think getting ready for this adventure was almost as much fun as the adventure itself. We read to each other in the evening and in the car on the way to the hard-ware store. We read everything we could get our hands on about cruising the world. We attended classes and seminars and talked with everyone we could who had sailed offshore. I was excited and scared.

The part that makes the dream so wonderful is your just dreaming. It's not reality yet. It's like diving off the high dive when you walk around the pool and wave to everyone. Then you climb the steps with such confidence. You look good, you feel excited and you're ready to jump, then you look down at the water and fear sets in. Its reality time and you've got to jump or risk being the fool. So you jump!

And so it is with the cruising adventure. There is always something to do on a boat and like a house, it's really never finished. So you set a date, you run around like a chicken and you invite all your friends to come wave good-bye and—you jump.

Bon Voyage

August 1, 1999 arrived with sunshine and my very nervous stomach. Our family and about 200 friends, neighbors and onlookers were there to say bon voyage. Our Japanese exchange daughter, Horoko, flew in all the way from Japan. Karen Thorndike, who had just completed a solo round-the-world voyage, was also there. The newspaper even sent a reporter.

The most difficult part for me was saying good-bye to my children and our seven-year-old grandson. My youngest daughter was crying so hard that the rose she brought to give me was wet with her tears. I kept that rose on the boat for almost four years, till it fell apart during a rough crossing out of New Zealand. I wondered if I would ever see my children again. I cried, they cried, everyone cried. Our grandson was busy collecting quarters from anyone who wanted a tour of the boat. He had quite a pocket full of quarters!

Eileen, a friend of ours, was busy collecting names and mailing addresses for the newsletter I would write and she would compile and mail out to everyone. It was called *Gone With the Wind* and it was sent out four times a year with articles and pictures of our adventure.

We finally untied the dock lines and hoisted the sails. About four or five other boats from the Everett Marina escorted us out of the harbor. One of our neighbor's sailboat had precious cargo—our children and grandson were sitting on deck waving their good-byes. Then we noticed everyone pointing at our boat. I thought they were just pointing out how awesome she looked. We finally looked behind us in the direction everyone was pointing. Our three-part nested dinghy we designed and built was no longer tethered to our sailboat. It was drifting in the harbor several yards behind Poet's Place. I guess I didn't learn knot tying as well as I thought! After much laughter, we turned around and retrieved our dinghy.

For our first night, we had decided to just sail across the bay to Whidbey Island where our friend Ruthie has a beautiful home. After setting anchor, we rowed our runaway dinghy to shore where Ruthie picked us up and drove us to her home for a lovely dinner. Another friend, Bridgett, was there to help. It was just what we needed after a long exciting day. At sunset, Ruthie drove us back to the bay where Poet's Place was waiting to rock us to sleep.

August 2nd was Steve's 53rd birthday (now we are both the same age - my birthday being in May). We had a good sail to Port Townsend where we picked up our crewmember, Tommy Hume (nephew of famous gardening expert, Ed Hume). Tommy is a good friend and seasoned sailor, who had done a number of offshore passages including the Southern Ocean. It was good to have his experience and help for the first leg of the trip to San Francisco. Steve and I had many discussions about taking crew with us on this journey. Steve wanted no one but the two of us and that sounded good to me except that I had zero experience on the open ocean. I heard terrifying stories about the open ocean, so I talked Steve into at least taking someone on this first leg to San Francisco to help ease my fear. I think it helped ease Steve also, although he would never admit it; my fear was a good excuse to have Tommy along. Tommy is the perfect crewmember. Not only is he an experienced sailor, he is also easy going and laid back with a great sense of humor. Tommy reminds me of a teddy bear, short and a bit roly-poly. You just want to hug him.

In Port Townsend we anchored next to Jeff and Mary, friends and dock neighbors from Everett marina. They gave us last minute advice and bid us fair winds. While there, we went into town to get ice-cream cones for Steve's birthday with new friends, Lane and Cheryl of S/V Halcyon. They will be leaving a week after us for a similar journey.

On August 3rd we left Port Townsend bound for Protection Island to meet our friends, Warren and Linda, at their cabin. With winds of 25 knots and no protection on Protection Island, we had to by-pass it and continue on to Port Angeles, waving to Warren and Linda as we sailed on by.

The wind picked up to 30 knots with the boat rail under water and crashing through six and seven foot waves. Steve was smiling, watching the boat perform so well. Tommy was ecstatic saying what a great sail it was. And I was complaining bitterly as I hate this point of sail. It was the only time during the entire trip to San Francisco that I felt queasy. I never had to use any of the many remedies I had on board for seasickness. Steve said I was too busy talking to get seasick.

As we were slogging along, I noticed our rugs were floating in wa-ter. Steve checked it out and discovered the bilge-pump drain was siphoning water in when we were laid hard over on a port tack. A lot of water was also coming over the bow and down our anchor chain pipe and into the bilge. Neither problem could be fixed until we got into calmer waters. I was not a happy camper. Finally, at 1:00 a.m. we anchored in Port Angeles, tired, hungry, cold and very wet. When I went into our clothes locker to get some dry clothes, I discovered all the clothes in our locker were soaked. I was already having second thoughts about this trip. A bus ticket home sounded good but I crashed and went to bed instead.

The next morning we emptied our clothes locker (while I com-plained the entire time) and filled several sail bags. It was all the three of us could do to lug those bags two miles through downtown Port Angeles looking like bag people, to the laundromat. Twelve loads later, we treated ourselves to a great Mexican lunch and a long hot shower at the marina. After that, I no longer thought about the bus ticket home. We spent three days in Port Angeles doing re-pairs on the boat and getting ready for the trip down the coast.

On day two, I decided to walk a few miles to the Safeway store to pick up a few items. Eight bags later I realized I could only carry one six pack of beer for Tommy. Being a recovery person myself and no longer a drinker, I reluctantly promised to keep him supplied with beer down the coast. When I returned from my grocery run, Tommy informed me he would never make it to San Francisco on one six pack. I promised him more beer at Neah Bay.

On August 6th we left Port Angeles at 5:00 a.m. to catch a good tide into Neah Bay (an Indian Reservation). How was I to know that Neah Bay was a "Dry Reservation"—no beer anywhere. I had no choice but to ration Tommy's beer; one for Cape Flattery, one when we cross into Oregon, one when we get to California, and so on, with the last one for the Golden Gate Bridge.

Saturday August 7th at 7:00 p.m. we left Neah Bay and sailed into the sunset headed to San Francisco. I was both excited and scared. We passed Cape Flattery lighthouse in flat seas and viewed the last sunset we would view until California. We sailed sixty miles offshore and by morning had a nice ten-knot breeze (the kind of sailing I love). Steve put out a fishing line, 200 pound test line with 150 pound test leader and an orange plastic squid lure. Within twenty minutes we had a twenty pound tuna on board. In one of the sailing magazines I had read that if you squirt some vodka (or any cheap liquor) down a fish's gills, it will die without a fight (and it's much more humane). When I got the vodka out to try this experiment, Tommy got a bit upset, suggesting I pour it down his gills instead of the fish. I ignored Tommy and inebriated the fish. It worked! We marinated the tuna steaks and grilled them on the barbeque. Boy is fresh tuna good. I don't know what they do to tuna in a can, but there's no comparison.

For most of the trip down the coast, we sailed sixty miles out, but at times we sailed eighty miles out. At eighty miles out, the water is a most beautiful shade of dark velvet blue, unlike the green blue at sixty miles out. Maybe that's what they mean when they say, *blue water sailing.*

Steve had built a self-steering vane which, when adjusted properly, allows the boat to steer itself. This is like autopilot on an airplane. Unfortunately, it wasn't finished when we left so we were hand steering all the way down the coast. I didn't know any different and just figured this was part of the work of sailing. Once he finished it in California, it made sailing the boat so easy and night watch more comfortable. I got so I couldn't live without it. But for now I was learning to hand steer.

Every morning, except on the last day, dolphins came to play and swim in our bow wake. It was an awesome sight. I would go out on the bow and talk with them. I got tired of talking with Steve and Tommy. Occasionally, we could see the dolphins swimming in the phosphorescence at night. It was a magical sight.

Night sailing can either be beautiful, as when the stars light up the heavens, or scary, as when the fog is thick and one sails through the middle of a fishing fleet, as we did. Glad we had radar to help us spot them.

The day after we caught the first tuna, we caught another one. We were still eating the first tuna, so I told the guys no more fishing until we finish eating what we have. Boy did we eat well. We finally had some sunshine on the fourth day out but it was still too cold for me. I lived in my long underwear and layers of clothes. The cabin temperature never got above 60 degrees, but then we never turned on the heater. We had enough hot air with Tommy and Steve aboard.

And then the storm hit on day seven and here I am, tired, scared and confused.

Maybe

Sharon Reed-Hendricks

Maybe you can't climb a mountain
Maybe it's too high
But for sure you'll never make it
If you never try

Maybe you can't swim with dolphins
The ocean's far away
You'll never know of the adventure
If you don't go someday

Maybe you can't live your dream out
For you have work to do
Well, you can wait for the right time
But time won't wait for you.

Maybe you can't change the world
The world won't change for you
Then maybe you can change yourself
And watch the world change too

Maybe you can't soar with eagles
And fly over the land
You'll never know unless you try
And maybe - you just can

2 California to Mexico

Sharon

By 5:00 a.m. we take turns napping for one hour each. We have all been awake for over twenty-four hours and are thoroughly exhausted. I saw fatigue as our biggest problem during the storm. When you are this tired, you don't think straight and mistakes happen. My job was to keep everyone fed and rested.

By 8:00 a.m. the seas and wind are much improved. The storm is over. It was one of the scariest nights of my life. We were too close to San Francisco for me to even think of turning around and heading back. I just wanted to get to dry land.

At 8:30 p.m. on Sunday August 15th, we sailed under the Golden Gate Bridge. It had taken us eight days and 961 miles. It was a thrill to sail Poet's Place all the way (and through a storm) from Everett, Washington to San Francisco, California. Of course the bridge was covered in fog, and until we sailed under it, I wasn't sure there was a bridge there at all. I told Tommy if I couldn't see the bridge then he didn't get his last beer. The look on his face had me rushing down below to the fridge!

We tied up at the San Francisco Municipal Marina where we had a view of the Golden Gate (when the fog cleared.) We finally set foot on solid ground for the first time in eight days. As we checked in with Joe, the night watchman, I asked about hot showers since I hadn't had one in ten days. Joe informed me that he had gone a whole year once without a shower. I told him ten days was long enough for me and I took one of my longest showers ever. After showering, we all crashed and no one woke until 10:30 a.m. the next day.

Once again we discovered that all of our clothing in the bottom locker was soaked. So once again, the three of us hauled our laundry this time, through downtown San Francisco. Only this time we found a Safeway grocery cart so we really did look like bag people. Doing laundry in San Francisco is a bit more expensive than Washington. Twenty five dollars later we had clean clothes.

We walk everywhere in San Francisco. We walk for groceries, boat parts, to the post office and all at different ends of town. It takes all day, but then we have all day to spend.

On Tuesday August 17th, after fourteen days with only six beers, we bid farewell to Tommy with mixed emotions. Steve and I needed our time alone, but we would really miss Tommy and his good humor. He was a great crewmember. We all went out for Chinese dinner in San Francisco before he left.

After saying good-bye to Tommy, Steve and I decided to get out of the San Francisco fog. We sailed over to Sausalito and anchored off this scenic town nestled in the hills. We stayed a few days and then left for Vallejo where we stayed at the yacht club. When you belong to a yacht club (or a sailing club as we did) and you travel out of the area, you have reciprocal privileges with many other yacht clubs. In other words, you can moor your boat at their yacht club for a night or two for free. You get a place to tie your boat, take hot showers and laundry; sometimes they even have a restaurant. We took full advantage of this reciprocal privilege. We were just going to stay overnight at the Vallejo Yacht Club, but stayed four nights instead. The people at the yacht club were very friendly. We had offers to take us anywhere we wanted to go - the wine country, the grocery store, or the hardware store. And Vallejo has one of the best farmers markets. For fifteen dollars we had nine bags of produce. Some ladies like to shop for shoes or jewelry. Not me, I like shopping for fruits and vegetables.

From Vallejo we went to the Delta, where the Sacramento and San Joaquin Rivers form the Delta area. One can actually sail all the way to Sacramento, but we didn't go that far. It's all river cruising and we loved it. I loved it here because the temperature was really warm. We swam every day, lay in the hammock, watched the sunset and rowed the dinghy around. This was heavenly. One day it got up to 116 degrees and I finally warmed up. Steve almost died. That night we slept in the cockpit naked. We soon had visitors—hordes of little black bugs and mosquitoes. All is not perfect in paradise! We got out the mosquito repellent and plastered it all over our bodies. They left us alone but stayed on the boat to Benicia, our next stop.

Benicia is a darling little town with a great farmers market. From there, we sailed to Angel Island (a real surprise) and anchored in China Cove, a beautiful anchorage with a spectacular view. On shore were the old deserted buildings from days of Chinese immigrations. We really explored the island and took a hike to Mt. Livermore. What a view from the top—all of San Francisco Bay and the surrounding area. We stayed for four days and hated to leave, but we had to tie up to a dock to do some much-needed repairs on the boat before heading down the coast. We sailed off to the Oakland Yacht Club where we stayed for another four days. The bathrooms at this yacht club were more like a hotel room. We met several members who were also heading south to Mexico and it was nice to talk with them. We made our repairs, did laundry, had our mail sent and found the farmers market. It was time to head down the coast to Mexico so we could arrive by November.

It was September 3rd and our first stop was Half Moon Bay, a very picturesque town. This was Labor Day weekend and we anchored in the bay with several other boats. We stayed two days, exploring the town before heading to Santa Cruz. We anchored off the town's old pier but the weather turned to gloom and doom and reminded me too much of Seattle. We left Santa Cruz after a day and sailed across the bay to Monterey.

It was a beautiful downwind sail, on a beautiful sunny day. It was one of those days when you're just happy to be alive. I looked at Steve and he smiled that smile at me. I was on the bow of the boat where Steve joined me; the wind vane steering (we named it Windy) was set and sailing the boat for us. Right there on the bow of our boat, on that beautiful day, we made love. What a way to get to Monterey.

We loved this place and enjoyed the many seals and sea lions. They were everywhere. We couldn't row our dinghy without bumping into one. One night we watched a magnificent lightning show from our cockpit. It rained all night and the next day the sun came out.

It was in Monterey that we met up with our friends Bob and Tikka and their son Andy, on their boat S/V *Harmony*. They were from our marina in Everett and left two weeks after we did. We were wondering where they were; it was great to see someone from home. We had dinner on their boat and we all decided to sail to San Simeon the next day. It was a sixteen-hour sail so we left at 4:00 a.m. We anchored under the lights of the Hearst Castle. It was magical.

San Simeon is where we learned, the hard way—to do dinghy landings in the surf. We heard later from others that few people ever land their dinghy there because the surf is so big. But Steve said we needed the practice even though I said no! For a few minutes our dinghy became a submarine. Everything was under water, including me. I was so mad. Our new digital camera was floating, our lunches were history and I never did find my sweatshirt or socks. Lucky for Steve our camera was still working. After bailing the water and sand from the dinghy and returning his less than happy wife back to *Poet's Place* to dry out our clothes, our fearless captain went back to the surf to practice. When he returned, he informed me he had dinghy surfing mastered. I really wanted to go ashore as there was an old Spanish mission and a beautiful beach beckoning me. I must be nuts, but I tried again. Over the waves we went like surfers and Steve said, "Get out when we hit the beach." All I heard was the "get out" and out I went into the water. Totally wet again, and there was Steve still dry in the dinghy. This time I brought a change of clothes in a water tight bag and changed on the beach. In spite of the surf, San Simeon continues to be one of my favorite anchorages in California.

From San Simeon, we sailed to Morrow Bay, which was one of Steve's favorite towns with its huge rock marking the entrance to the bay. We stayed three days before heading to San Luis Obispo for a night of rest, before an overnight sail to round the famous Cape Conception. We needed to avoid rounding the cape in the afternoon when winds can reach up to 40 knots, so we had to time it for early morning, which meant sailing all night. We rounded the cape with no wind and lumpy seas. We were headed for the Channel Islands and arrived at San Miguel Island at 8:00 a.m. What a beauty. The Channel Islands are like the Galapagos of California. Unbelievable! From the face-powder fine sand beaches of San Miguel where I collected sand dollars and sea shells, to the painted caves of Santa Cruz. At anchor we could see down twenty feet, to view crystal clear waters with bright blue, orange and red fish swimming. It was like looking into an aquarium.

Steve
We rowed our dinghy into Painted Cave, where the entrance was eighty feet and rose to one-hundred-thirty feet high inside. Beautiful reds, greens and blues glowed in the low lights as one entered the cave. As we rowed our dinghy into the cave there was about a three-foot swell running. As the swell pushed into the cave the water surged through many side caves causing a steady loud rumbling noise like thunder. We rowed further in and the noise grew louder and louder. It was beautiful and scary at the same time. We were about 400 feet inside the main cave and the ceiling was eight feet above our head and coming down closer as each swell raised us close enough to touch the mosaic colored limestone. At this point the cave made a 90-degree turn to the right into a black tunnel about twelve feet wide and six feet from water to ceiling. At this point we had a little discussion about the wisdom of exploring further. We had to shout to be heard over the thunderous noise. I said we have come this far, lets see where it goes. We had brought a small flashlight that dimly lit the way. We felt like we were on the wildest carnival ride we had ever experienced! We were pitching

21

up and down in the dark, water dripping from the ceiling like rain, the air trembling from the roar of thousands of tons of water coursing through the passageways, slipping deeper and deeper into an unknown black hole. Finally, another two hundred feet into this pitch black hole we washed into a larger room about forty feet in diameter. It seemed like the end of the cave with a raised ledge all along the wall. We just sat there a minute to marvel at what nature had created here. As our eyes adjusted more to the darkness, we shined our little flashlight around at the rocks and were surprised that some of the rocks had glowing eyes staring back at us. We suddenly realized we were surrounded by sea lions. Sharon said, "I am scared, let's get out of here." Then our little flashlight batteries died. There we were about 600 feet in a cave so dark we could not see anything. We could kind of tell by the sound of the water rumbling through the main tunnel the direction we needed to go to find our way out. Outside the sea lion den we could see a faint light that showed the way out. What a beautiful, exciting and scary place to explore. We were happy to get out and glad we took the time to explore this wondrous work of nature.

Sharon
Outside, sea lions and seals jumping next to our boat for hours at a time entertained us. We watched wild pigs on the beach while we ate our breakfast in the cockpit and again in the evening while we ate dinner. We sailed into a pod of over one-hundred pilot whales that were frolicking in the water. We slowed down to watch and take pictures. We hated to leave this place, but we needed to head to San Diego to do more repairs before heading to Mexico, and I needed another farmer's market.

Steve
San Diego was a memorable stop; we pulled into the Police Dock to see if we could get a slip at the public docks. They said there was one slip left way at the end of the fairway. It was really too windy to try this maneuver but we were naive, so we decided to try. The wind was blowing 25 knots from our port stern quarter. We were picking up speed down the fairway at an alarming rate so I

shifted into reverse to slow us down but then the wind was pushing us sideways into the sterns of other boats berthed along the fairway. With disaster pending, I left the helm to fend us off of the other boats. I commanded Sharon to take over the helm and give it more power to back away from the boats, as I push off of a couple about to scrape our side. We were doing much better backing away, then I looked behind us and saw a forty-six foot boat parked in a 25-foot slip sticking way out from the docks. We were now full speed, in reverse, bearing down on the forty-six footer. At which point I rushed to our stern while shouting to Sharon "FORWARD!" Sharon grabbed the shift lever and went from full power reverse to full power forward in one swift move. The transmission groaned, the engine roared, smoke billowed out and water churned. Just as we were about to smash the other boat the captain of the 46 footer came on deck to see what all the commotion was about. With terror in his eyes he put his sandwich in his mouth, braced for the impact and leaned forward to try to fend us off. At this moment I was face to face with him. We were both reaching out to fend off the imminent collision when our propeller caught traction and changed our fate and our direction. At which point the captain, with his sandwich in his mouth, lost his balance and promptly fell into the water. I had no time to see if he ever came up as I raced back to the helm and instructed Sharon to get dock lines ready to throw. By this time everyone in the marina was out on the dock watching the chaos; we had plenty of help as we drifted into our slip. After we were tied up we just went below, too embarrassed to show our face on the dock for a while. We learned a lot that day, hugged each other and vowed to stay out of marinas as much as possible.

Sharon

We had made every stop possible sailing down the California coast. Reaching San Diego was a milestone for us. We had sailed Poet's Place from the northern most tip of the continental U.S. to the southernmost tip. We spent two weeks in San Diego before heading to Mexico and had several visitors, including daughter Tracy and grandson Cody. While there, we visited the San Diego Zoo and Sea World.

We left San Diego on November 1st at 3:00 a.m., arriving that evening in Ensenada, Mexico. November 2nd was a holiday in Mexico (everyday seems to be a holiday here) and all government offices were closed. That meant we had to wait until the following day to do our check-in. We spent the day exploring the town. The next day we did what I call the Mexican Cha-Cha (checking into the country). This in itself is an experience. At 8:30 a.m., we rowed our dinghy from our anchorage to the dinghy dock. We walked about a mile to the immigration office where we needed six copies of our crew list in Spanish. I had some already done on our computer, complete with photos. This was over-kill, since they insisted it be filled out on their forms only. I'm sure the immigration's officer took pity upon me when he saw the look on my face as he got out the manual typewriter and started to put together six forms and five sheets of carbon and started typing. He was smiling and asking questions in Spanish. This took awhile since my Spanish was not the greatest. Next, we had to take the six forms to the Port Captains office down the street. The sweet girl in the front office looked at the forms and asked (in Spanish, of course) where our receipt was. We, being dumb gringos, knew nothing about a receipt. She informed us it had something to do with an anchoring fee or a Marina fee. We had neither form, but we did have one for the dinghy dock back on the boat. Since she insisted on a receipt, we walked back to the dinghy dock, rowed back to the boat, picked up one dinghy dock receipt, rowed back and walked into town—again. After waiting in line for our turn, we finally presented our receipt. She seemed satisfied, stamped all six copies like she was using a sledge hammer, smiled and said, "*Uno momento*"(one minute). A half hour later she returned, smiled and handed us back our six copies signed by the Port Captain. We then took the copies back to immigration where we waited in line for them to take six copies and give us back four copies. We then took these to the bank on the other end of town to wait in another line to pay the $15 fee for the visa stamp. Now, we were officially checked into the country. All of this took only four and a half hours. You get to go through something similar at every major port. Some cruisers hate the time this takes and actual-

24

ly pay someone to do this for them. I'm a tightwad, and besides, I found the experience worth every minute. We meet lots of other people while waiting in line (both cruisers and locals), and we get to find our way around town and practice our Spanish.

We only stayed two days in Ensenada and it was the last time I would see a bank, large grocery store, or laundromat, until we reached Cabo San Lucas, 892 miles and one month later.

From Ensenada, we sailed to Punta Colnett, then on to Isla San Martin. Isla San Martin is a remnant of an extinct volcano. On the way, we caught a nice ten-pound tuna. As soon as we anchored, a panga (rowboat) with a fisherman, his young wife, and two year old son came out to our boat. Elizabeth, the wife, spoke English, her husband Martin spoke only Spanish, and their two year old didn't speak at all. Elizabeth invited herself on our boat. She was excited because she had never been on a sailboat before. After cookies and coffee, and more cookies, and again more cookies, I suggested we visit their island. Ashore, Elizabeth welcomed us to their modest one room, dirt floor home in the small fishing village. I think what surprised me the most was the garbage system at the village. There was none. They just throw the garbage out the window or door, and it lands wherever.

I made a suggestion that burying or burning was a good way to take care of garbage. Elizabeth agreed with me as she threw the disposable diaper out the window. Steve says it solves the problem of who's to take out the garbage. He also likes the dirt floor idea—no vacuuming or worrying about spills on the carpet. While on the island, I gave Steve a haircut then Elizabeth asked if I would cut her husband's hair. I did, and they said it was the best haircut he has ever had. I guess I could get a job as a barber in Mexico. Later, we all hiked to the top of the volcano. It was awesome! Before returning to our boat, Elizabeth and Martin gave us squid, snails and fish and Elizabeth made us homemade tortillas. What an experience!

The next day we sailed to Cabo San Quintin where we anchored in

25

25 knots of wind. We sailed all the next day and night in 35 knots of wind and big seas. It's times like these, that I wonder why I'm doing this. Then we arrive at Cedros Island in the warm sunshine and anchored in crystal clear water off a beach that is home to over 1000 sea lions and elephant seals, and I know why. Several of the sea lions came out to the boat to welcome us. They performed their water ballet while we took solar showers in the cockpit. The next day, Steve and I decided to go snorkeling and rowed to the next beach so as not to disturb the sea lions. Some of the babies followed us; as we snorkeled they swam with us. At times they would swim under us and look up at us.

After Cedros, we sailed to San Benitos, a group of three islands. We had some problems with our old Atomic Four engine as we approached the islands at dusk. Our sailing skills were tested as we anchored under sail in the dark. Steve worked all the next day on the engine; it turned out we needed new spark plugs. Lucky we carry back up parts with us. Here in San Benitos, we traded local fishermen (something we would do quite often in Mexico) three cans of pop and a pack of gum for four nice lobsters.

We left San Benitos and had a nice downwind sail to Turtle Bay. While at anchor at Turtle Bay we saw our friends, on the sailboat *Harmony*, from our marina back home. It was a nice reunion. Turtle Bay is an interesting place with a challenging pier. We climbed the rusty, steep ladder about fourteen feet to the top where we stepped onto another rusty area that bridges the ladder to the wood pier with a space large enough for one's body to drop through. After doing the split from the top of the ladder across the rusty platform to the wood, we were now safely on the pier. When transporting groceries or laundry, a long rope came in handy for lowering and lifting from the dinghy to the pier.

As soon as we stepped foot on the pier we were met by Miguel, the local Chamber of Commerce/self-appointed tour guide. He led us all over town, and in broken English pointed out all the sights. The town is not very large, has all dirt roads, no telephones and many businesses are closed or nonexistent. Miguel's favorite word to describe these conditions was "broke." We asked him about the empty cannery building at the pier, "broke." The bank, "broke." The laundromat, "broke." He let us know that if we had laundry, his wife would do it *"manana"*. Throughout this tour Miguel keeps asking us if we would like to go to a good restaurant. We kept telling him "later", until finally we said yes just to keep him quiet. Down the street, into the little restaurant Miguel found us a table and promptly sat himself down. We ordered. He ordered. I looked at Steve. Steve looked at me. We were thinking the same thing. Who pays Miguel's bill? Luckily the prices were cheap, about three dollars each, except Miguel's. His was four dollars. We figured it was worth the experience.

The next day, after hauling laundry up the pier and negotiating a price with Miguel and meeting his wife, we and another couple decided to try a new restaurant, while waiting for our laundry. A busty Mexican glamour queen ran this one. No kidding, a bleached blond with a very low-cut black dress to show off her very large breast. She was really very nice and when she brought out the dominos for us, we knew this was a clue that lunch would take awhile. Across the street she went to get the tortillas, down the street to the store to get our drinks and back to the house to get the vegetables. Hey, we have more time than money now, so this was an experience. Anyway, lunch was great and the laundry turned out clean. We even got an extra T-shirt that wasn't ours. We think after they saw our shabby and stained clothes, they felt sorry for us and threw in an extra shirt—just Steve's size.

While in Turtle Bay, I became very popular with the kids as I gave away colorful pens. It doesn't take long at all; you give out a couple of pens to a couple of kids and within minutes every kid in the village is following you around town asking for a pen. We really enjoyed Turtle Bay and its colorful people, but it was getting cooler and it was time to head south. We left Turtle Bay a 4:00 a.m. surrounded by a magnificent meteor shower. It was awesome.

We sailed to Bahia Asuncion then to Punta Abreojos. These were long grueling days, up at 2:00 a.m. to anchor before dark, and then up again to do it all over. Then we had a two-day two- night sail to Bahia Santa Maria in twenty-five knot winds and ten-foot seas the whole time. Not comfortable, but we've seen worse. Bahia Santa Maria was a beautiful anchorage with a nice beach and great swimming. We stayed three days before sailing the twenty-five miles to Magdalena Bay where we spent Thanksgiving week. We fell in love with this little village of 300 (250 of them kids). While restocking produce there, I inquired about fresh tortillas. A young girl of about twelve, who helped at the little market, took off and quickly returned to tell me, "Mama make a tortillas." She took my hand and led me, along with Steve, up the hill to her little casa where Mama, three little sisters and Papa were waiting. No one spoke English. Somehow, with my limited Spanish we got by. That night I learned to make tortillas. Of course the ones I made looked nothing like the ones Mama made. Thirty-six tortillas later I asked how many pesos, Mama crossed her arms and said no. While I was busy making tortillas, Steve was drinking coffee with Papa and telling him all about our feast of Thanksgiving which was the next day. Papa is a lobster diver and invited us to their home for a lobster Thanksgiving fiesta. We asked if we could bring our friends Jean and Blase on *S/V Paraclete,* whom we were going to share Thanksgiving dinner with. We said we'd all bring food to share.

On Thanksgiving morning, I was invited to visit the school (it's not a holiday here). I was getting very popular again with the kids as I gave away more pens. Giving out candy also works. I think the school's pen supply was low. The school consisted of two classrooms, one for the younger kids, and one for the older kids. They sit wherever they are comfortable; on the floor, on top of the desk, hanging out the window—wherever. If they can't see the blackboard, well no problem, just stand on their desk or someone else's. None of this ever bothers the teacher. She just keeps on teaching. The average American teacher would have heart failure. I wish I had gone to a school like this. They all seem to be having so much fun.

28

That afternoon, Steve and I along with Jean and Blase, a cruising couple we met in California, gathered our food and made our way to the lobster diver's casa. Sure enough, they had lobster ready. We had quite a feast. Jean made a rather large pumpkin pie and when it came time for dessert, several kids showed up. Jean even brought her piano (a Costco portable special), as she use to be a piano teacher. When the music started, more kids arrived, until I'm sure every kid in the village was there. We sang *Old McDonald* with the help of my big Spanish picture book. I even did the Mexican Hat Dance with one of the teenage boys. Steve said we turned that poor Mama's casa into a Mexican Fiesta. We were all exhausted.

To some people, this little Mexican village looks like the people have so little, yet to me they have so much. They have no vehicles except a couple of old trucks (there are really no roads), no traffic jams, no busy malls, no fast food, no television. Families have time to watch the stars at night. I watched mom's hanging out laundry and greeting their children as they ran home from school. I felt as if I had stepped back in time. Everyone was friendly and happy. There was no rushing, no stress. I wonder sometimes what we've done in our modem society trading peacefulness and slow pace for busy polluted cities and stress.

We hated to leave this lovely village, but we had kids to meet in Cabo San Lucas and we had a two day - two night sail to get there. We caught another nice tuna on the way to Cabo and the water temperature warmed up to 80 degrees. In Cabo, we anchored off the busy beach in clear warm water. We were able to jump off the boat and swim or snorkel every day. One day, Steve and I rented a motor scooter to tour the area. On another day, I got to visit the dentist, as I needed a filling. The dentist spoke English and did a great job for 300 pesos (about $30).

On November 30th our daughter Tracy, her friend Mike, our eight-year-old grandson Cody, daughter Michelle and nephew Jeff, all arrived in Cabo for a week of fun and sun. Cody stayed on the boat with us because, as he puts it, "It's boring in the hotel with the adults"(a real compliment to young grandparents). We all had a great reunion in Cabo and the best way to describe it is to share some of Cody's journal.

Cody's Journal:

11-30-99   I flew on a plane to Mexico. Then we rowed out to Grandpa's sailboat and we ate popcorn. I took a solar shower.

12-1-99   We ate pancakes with bananas. We jumped off the boat and a jellyfish stung me. And we rowed over to a rusty fishing boat and bought shrimp. Then we made a sand castle on the beach. And we lay in the hammock on the boat. And I love Mexican papaya.

12-2-99   Today we picked up my friend Andy who lives on the boat *Harmony* and we went to Lover's Beach. We went swimming and saw flying fish. Played cards with Grandpa and got all the money.

12-3-99   Today we went to town to buy fruit. We ate tacos for lunch and we bought fresh hot tortias. Jumped off the boat and ate popcorn and made brownies, too. And found a surfboard.

12-4-99   I caught a humongous fish and ate ten tortias and caught six swordfish all in a net. I played with my friend Andy. I played cards and watched fireworks.

12-5-99   I ate more tortias. We went sailing. Surfed and jumped off the boat and I saw a fish. I played in the sand at Lover's Beach.

Sharon

It was sad to say goodbye to the kids, but as long as they keep coming to visit, I won't have a chance to get too homesick. Next stop was Los Frailes, about forty-five miles northeast of Cabo San Lucas and into the Sea of Cortez. This was a beautiful anchorage with crystal clear water, beautiful sandy beaches and the best snorkeling so far. I saw so many colorful fish. It was like swimming in an aquarium. It was hard to believe it was December. The weather conditions outside the anchorage at Los Frailes were not good for several days. High winds and seas had us waiting for a good weather window to make the crossing to Mazatlan on the mainland of Mexico. We decided not to go any farther into the Sea of Cortez this time of the year because it tends to be cold. We may come back and do the Sea this spring. There were four boats waiting to leave the anchorage and we kept in radio contact. We even had a potluck dinner on one of the larger boats and played a game that had us laughing so hard our insides hurt. Finally the weather improved some, so everyone left to go in a different direction. Instead of goodbye we say "till we meet again," because when you're cruising you keep meeting up with these people again, but you never know where or when.

The crossing to Mazatlan was a rough and uncomfortable passage. We encountered 25 knots of wind and rolling seas. After two days and two nights we arrived in Mazatlan, where we stayed for two weeks through Christmas. Friends, Sharon and John Townsell, from Everett, helped to make our stay there a very pleasant one by taking us all over and showing us everything. We spent a lovely Christmas Eve and Christmas day with them. They live there six months out of the year and we learned why they love it so much. While in Mazatlan we experienced some engine problems and had to order a head gasket and exhaust valve, which we will pick up in Puerto Vallarta. Steve will be busy when we get there.

On December 26th we left Mazatlan to sail to San Bias. On the way we stopped at Isla Isabela, another experience of a lifetime. The lush jungle island is a bird sanctuary and home to thousands of frigate birds, blue-footed boobies, terns and gulls. We rowed our dinghy ashore to the fishing village and some young boys showed us the trail through the jungle. We hiked up a hill, through a banana grove (I picked a month's worth of bananas) and past a picturesque lake, where we stopped for lunch. After lunch, we hiked passed the iguanas (lizards) that were over three feet long (they don't like their picture taken). We were completely surrounded by bushes with nesting frigate birds. The bushes were at eye level and many of the nests had white fuzzy babies. I guess they only hatch one baby at a time. We were within a foot of their nests and they didn't seem to mind us taking pictures. I restrained from touching the babies when

I saw mama keeping a sharp eye (and beak) on me. We also got to observe, up close and personal, blue-footed boobies and their babies. These birds really have mint green webbed feet, not blue.

We sailed to San Blas and anchored in the river estuary. If you've ever seen the movie *African Queen*, you'll know what it looks like. While in San Blas we went on a jungle river ride in a panga with our friends, Jean and Blase, on the boat *Paraclete* (I told you we keep meeting up with these cruisers). This was some jungle ride. We saw birds of every color, crocodiles, turtles and even a boa constrictor hanging from a tree. There were wild orchards in the trees, lilies and beautiful flowers everywhere. Even thatched roof huts on stilts in the river. We stopped for lunch at a crystal clear fresh water spring complete with a vine to swing Tarzan style into the deep pond. We all swam in the surprisingly warm water until the ten-foot crocodile, which was watching us from a rock, decided to slide in and join us. When a crocodile wants the pond to himself—he gets it! You never saw four people jump out of the water so fast as when he smiled and showed us his teeth. It was a day we will never forget. Steve and Blase are still sore from swinging off that vine (we're not as young as we think we are).

We fell in love with this quaint little Mexican town and its people in the week that we were there. I lost another filling while in San Bias (must be the tortillas) so I had to go to the dentist. This one spoke very little English and did an excellent job for 100 pesos (about $10). Going to the dentist in Mexico is like it was fifty years ago in the U.S. Same equipment we had back then, no insurance to deal with, no assistant, no overhead (they usually work out of their homes) and no high prices. We are now in La Cruz / Puerto Vallarta area where we will pick up our Christmas mail in January and do a valve job on the engine before heading south. We are trying to decide if we will continue on to Costa Rica this summer or go back into the Sea of Cortez and do Costa Rica next spring. To Sea or not to Sea, that is the question. These are tough decisions—where in paradise to go next. It's a tough life, but somebody has got to do it.

Follow Your Dream

Sharon Reed-Hendricks

Listen to your spirit
The voice that's deep inside
Follow each and every dream
Your spirit is your guide

Let your spirit guide you
You will find its helping hand
Follow each and every dream
Though you may not understand

Feel the spirit move you
To a place you need to be
Follow each and every dream
You'll soon begin to see

Trust your spirit's wisdom
It is always right and true
Follow each and every dream
And you'll find the dream for you

3   Mexico

Sharon

Our plans to continue south this year have been completely de-railed by the pleasures and beauty of the *Sea of Cortez*. The beauty of the cruising life is that you don't have to stick to any plan—and we're sure sticking to that!

If we were to describe Mexico in one word, it would be colorful—the countryside, the people and the food. We didn't want to miss any of it, so we slowed down to smell the tortillas and see the sea while we are here. Who knows when we'll be this way again. But before we continued to the Sea of Cortez we had things to do and more places to go.

We stayed in La Cruz; about ten miles south of Puerto Vallarta, at anchor for a month while Steve re-built the engine. We are lucky in that we never have to start our engine to recharge our batteries. It confirmed the good decision we had made by having solar panels on our boat. We have two 120-watt Photocom solar panels mounted on a stainless steel arch, which Steve welded to hold them in place. These panels keep our four house batteries charged which takes care of all our electrical needs. This includes our re-frigerator, water-maker, ham radio, computer, fans and all our lights. Plus, we have no electric bill.

We really loved La Cruz. It is a quaint little town with cobble-stone streets, a town square and almost everything we need can be found in one of the little tiendas (stores). They even have an ice cream tienda. It is almost untouched by tourism (not a pay phone in the whole town) and only a ten-mile bus ride into Puerto Val-larta.

Speaking of bus rides—this is a must if you visit Mexico. The drivers have a little more freedom here and can decorate their buses any way they choose. This usually consists of a religious picture of the Madonna next to a pin-up of a sexy model, along with lots of other colorful decorations. A frame of fringe or "dingo balls" around the ceiling of the bus completes the decor. Often, there is a large or giant boom box next to the driver for your listening pleasure (bring ear plugs). This boom box is turned to "high" volume with the driver's favorite Mexican tunes blasting while the bus sways back and forth down the road at 70-80 miles per hour to the rhythm of the music. The drivers (age 14-75) are *kamikaze wannabes*. The ride is wild! Steve thinks it's better than any Disneyland ride. Sometimes they pick up a singer or a guitar player and they perform in the aisle while the bus is zooming down the road. Some are quite good. (Back home they would lock them up).

After La Cruz we sailed around the dreaded Cabo Corrientes (we did fine) to Punta Ipala. This is a small village where the welcoming committees of young boys swim out to your boat to greet you and ask for school supplies. With my pen supply and zip lock bags (I'm not sure how they expected to keep them dry), we made friends quickly.

Bahia Chamela was our next stop, where we went around the corner to Isla Colorado where we found a little cove with some of the best snorkeling so far. It looked like something out of one of those travel brochures; white sandy beach, crystal clear turquoise water and colorful fish. We had it all to ourselves. Then our friends on *Paraclete* radioed us to see where we were and when we told them about this place, they immediately hauled anchor in PV (Puerto Vallarta) and headed for Isla Colorado. Trouble is, the VHF radio is like the old fashion telephone party lines and any boat within radio reach can hear your conversation! Within two days, our "private island" became a small city, with eight other boats. Everyone agreed it was a most beautiful spot.

Next stop was Careyes, the "Riviera" of Mexico, with its brightly colored bungalows (looking like colored Easter eggs) set in the hillside surrounded by flowers with coconut palms swaying in the breeze on the beach below. It was a sight to behold. We went ashore to the beach in front of the Belair Hotel and walked around, bought some items from their deli, then sat around the pool where the maid brought us heated towels to dry off. This is the way to enjoy "hotel cruising." The hotel didn't seem to mind our using their pool as long as we bought a drink or food item.

On to Tenacatita, one of the most beautiful and tranquil anchorage's in this part of the coast. There were about thirty boats anchored there when we arrived in early February, just in time for the potluck on the beach. I think we knew about twenty of the boats there, some we had not seen since California. It was like old home week and I loved it. This is where we met up with Darrell and Sandy of S/V *Black Swan* from our marina in Everett. Although we had never met them before, we were told to look for them in Mexico. The potluck was to celebrate Darrell's birthday. We also ran into Tony Keeling and his wife Linda on S/V *Veritas*. He's an old friend of Steve's who he hadn't seen for over fifteen years. Steve had heard that he was off sailing "somewhere," so what a surprise for them to run into each other here. We had great times with many friends at this wonderful anchorage.

A favorite past time of cruisers is landing a dinghy in the surf, which is as wild as any jungle ride. Several cruisers would sit at the palapa on the beach and watch other cruisers crash through the surf. They would then rate them on a scale of 1-10 on performance. This would get pretty funny at times. Nearby, we discovered a French restaurant on the beach surrounded by coconut palms. It was the setting for the movie *McHale's Navy*. Imagine that.

Next we sailed to what we called "Rocky Melague" (pronounced Mel-lock-key), a darling town, and then to Barra de Navidad just a few miles south. We anchored in the lagoon in Barra which can be a real challenge going through the entrance. We promptly went aground (sand bottom) and had to wait for fellow cruisers to help pull us off.

In Barra, there is the low-rent district (the lagoon) and the high-rent district (marina off the fancy hotel). We were in the low-rent district, but had friends staying in the high-rent district. The high-renters could have "guests" visit and swim in the hotel's several pools, so on any given day, everyone from the lagoon could be found frolicking at the hotel's pools. Waterfalls and slides connected the pools. They were great fun, but one sure needed tight-fitting swimwear. A few ladies lost their bathing suit tops while zooming down the slide (no names mentioned). This provided much entertainment for the crowd and embarrassment for the ladies. We had a tour of the hotel while we were there and it is unbelievable! I've never seen anything like it in my life. It is truly *grande*.

It was while in Barra, that we decided to turn back north and sail the Sea of Cortez for the summer. Costa Rica will have to wait until next year. So many other cruisers we met told us how beautiful the "Sea" was, so we decided if we didn't do it now, who knows when we'd be this way again. So that's what we did.

Cruising is always saying goodbye. Leaving Barra was a bitter-sweet time for the cruising fleet because many of our cruising friends continued south into Costa Rica and Panama. Others went through the canal to the Caribbean or to the South Pacific, back home to the States or to the *"Sea"* for the summer. Who knows when or where, we would see any of them again.

It seemed strange heading north, almost like going home and I wasn't ready for that yet, even though I've threatened several times. Heading north is not ideal as the winds are usually out of the north; bashing into wind and seas is not my idea of fun. We experienced some bashing seas but we also had some good passages as we re-traced our steps back north.

Steve
A most interesting island visited in our northbound travels was Isla La Marina in Banderas Bay, where we went exploring with friends, Jeannie and Blase and their faithful dog, Curly. The shore-

38

line of the island is all high cliffs, but we managed to find one spot where we could land our dinghies and climb up the rock to get onto the main part of the island. Because this way is difficult and hard to find, very few people ever go on the island. The trails on the island are made by the resident booby birds and are hard to follow plus there are blue-footed boobies everywhere one steps. It was a little like going through a maze to get anywhere. We climbed up about fifty feet through rock rubble and booby birds to find the entrance to a cave. We were amazed to find the cave was quite large inside with a big room maybe seventy feet across and fifty feet high. The walls and ceiling were a beautiful mosaic of colored limestone and ancient coral. There was a dark passageway about six feet wide in the back of the cave going off in another direction. There was very little sign of people ever visiting this cave except for a ring of stones marking an old campfire. Except for the damp moss-covered floor it looked like a good place to live. After marveling at this great creation of nature, we decided to explore the dark passageway. Fifty feet into the tunnel our eyes adjusted to the dark and we could see light coming from the other end. Another two-hundred feet or so we came out the other side of the island and upon a magnificent view of another large plateau area looking west out over the blue Pacific.

From here, we climbed along the rock and found two more similar caves. In the large cave, the main room was about one-hundred-twenty feet across, the ceiling sixty feet high and there were six different tunnels leading out in six different directions with magnificent views in all directions. This cave obviously had inhabitants at one time. There were crude steps carved in the rock leading to different levels in the cave. Religious type altars were set up in two different spots. Rocks were placed on the floor in strange patterns. While it was a most beautiful place to visit, it also gave us a very eerie feeling as we wondered just what kind of people had lived here and when. Was it one person or a hermit? Maybe it was pirates? Or, was it a whole tribe of Indians? Perhaps it was a religious cult. We had only explored about half the island and we knew there were more caves on the other half but that would have to wait until the next time we visit Isla.

Sharon

Our next stop was Chacala, a charming village where the beach is lined with coconut palms and a welcoming committee of young boys who swam out to our boat. This is also where we had our first (and last for me) hitchhiking experience in Mexico. It all started out so innocently. We were dressed for the beach, bathing suits and T-shirts and very little money as we were going for a short walk. As we were walking along the dirt road, a pick-up driven by a nice young local, stopped to offer us a ride. Steve immediately said *si* over my *no, gracias* and I was quickly escorted into the front seat of the pickup. We started talking, and next thing I knew, the little dirt road had turned into a big highway. I asked where we were going and Steve said to relax and enjoy the adventure. I then asked our chauffeur *"Donde estamos"*? He smiled and said the name of some town I had never heard of.

When we arrived in this rather large town, I asked if we should wait for our driver or take a bus back to Chacala. Our driver said there was no bus and he goes back *manana*. When I looked at Steve, he smiled and said, (much to my horror) "We'll just hitchhike back." We weren't exactly dressed for town, so after browsing around we ventured out to the highway. The day was hot, about 90 degrees, as we stuck out our thumbs toward Chacala. I obviously was not in practice as several cars zoomed by at about 70 mph. Finally a new Chevy pick-up screeched to a stop and two young men motioned to us to squeeze in the already crowded front seat. We were barely inside when the truck screeched and zoomed down the highway at 95 mph. It wasn't until we were inside the truck that we realized the two men were drunk as skunks and still drinking while we were tearing down the highway at the speed of light! They offered us a beer (Steve says he should have taken one just to settle his nerves). Believe me when I say that sailing the high seas in a full gale is mild compared to this ride! They passed every car on the highway, right into head-on traffic coming the other way. I've never been this scared, not even the "storm from hell"

40

created such terror. Finally Steve shouted, "STOP," as I was too scared to talk (if you can believe that). We got out of the truck but didn't know where we were, but that didn't matter. We were still alive. We looked around the deserted highway and walked to a lone tienda to ask how far to Chacala. We found out we were ten miles past the turnoff to the road that leads into Chacala. Back to the highway, thumbs out in the other direction, in 95 degree heat, I was NOT a happy hitchhiker. Finally, after about an hour of sun-burned thumbs, a nice middle-aged Mexican man stopped and drove us the ten miles back to the turnoff to Chacala. This was a dusty country dirt road, but I'll have to admit the scenery was breathtaking. Mango, banana, papaya and coconut palm trees were everywhere. The mountains in the background were lush and green and everywhere I looked there were little ranches with horses and cattle. It was eight miles back to town and I would have en-joyed the walk if it weren't so far.

Luckily an old truck loaded with bricks and driven by two weath-ered Mexicans stopped and motioned for us to hop in the back with the bricks. As we traveled down this dirt road, each and every time we hit a bump, the spaces between the bricks smacked to-gether pinching my behind. We finally drove into town with all the locals and cruisers looking on. Steve thought this was a great adventure.

As we continued north, we once again stopped in San Bias and an-chored up the estuary jungle river, one of our many favorite places. When we were here before, we befriended several of the locals, so Steve was able to use the palapa workshop of one of the local fish-ermen to build our cockpit bed. It's great to have a place to sleep outside, under the stars, on these warm summer nights. While in San Bias we made an inland trip by bus with another cruising cou-ple to Tepic. The scenery through the mountains was spectacular!

We made it to Mazatlan in two days (takes most cruisers one day because they motor); we love to sail and the wind is free. We had lots of paperwork to do there as our six-month visas were about to expire and we needed to obtain what's called a FM3 to extend our stay in Mexico. We really put our folding bikes to good use in Mazatlan riding back and forth to immigration almost every day. We also visited once again with friends, John and Sharon Townsell, from Everett, who live here six months out of the year. We had a wonderful time.

Mexico loves paperwork. The process of obtaining a FM3 involves volumes of work. This process is time consuming and a little mind-boggling. There are several forms, each of them needing six copies, which must he typed (in Spanish, of course). One also needs photos (front and side), letters, references and money (and lots of patience). A person can wait three weeks or more for this process to complete and then one can stay in the country another year. Our friends the Townsells, were a great help. Spending much of our time at immigration, we befriended Dora, the immigration's lady who was extremely helpful and very charming. She and I both like to talk (surprise) and gather information about different cultures. She asked lots of questions about the boat and I asked her if she had ever been on a sailboat. When she said no, I asked if she would like to visit ours and bring her family. Her smile told me her answer. On Saturday, Dora and her two children came to visit and we had a wonderful time. She got a little seasick, but loved it just the same. Her children were delightful. We found out that in the twenty-three years Dora has worked in immigrations, no one had ever invited her onto their boat. Before she left the boat, she asked us to come get our FM3's on Wednesday, after only a one week wait. The other cruisers, who had been waiting for over three weeks, gave us a funny look when we walked into immigrations and Dora got up from her desk, came over and gave us a big hug and handed us our FM3's. "How do you rate?" they asked. A little bit of friendship goes a long way!

The passage from Mazatlan across the Sea of Cortez to La Paz takes most cruisers two days. We had a wonderful four-day four-night light wind passage and sailed the entire way. One day we were becalmed for eight hours in the most beautiful crystal clear blue water with about a hundred feet of visibility. We saw many colorful fish swimming beneath the boat. We also saw two big sea turtles swimming circles around us. Then the dolphins came; not only did we see them when they jumped next to our bow, but we could see them swimming fifty feet below. We saw every mark on their bodies. What an awesome sight! It was like we were sailing in an aquarium.

The boat wasn't moving and the temperature was about 90 degrees outside, so we took off our clothes and jumped into the beautiful blue water. We were like little kids playing in a pool. It was a strange feeling swimming with two thousand five hundred feet of water beneath you. By the end of the day we had a new crew-member in the form of a little yellow canary. He flew on board and into the cabin, resting on my teddy bears and not wanting to leave. A little later he flew back to the cockpit and onto my foot as his perch. After a few hours inspection of the boat, he flew away. It was a most magical day, the kind you dream about.

A few days later we arrived at Isla Espiritu Santo and dropped the hook in the crystal clear turquoise water. We had arrived in the Sea. After a few days of rest we headed to La Paz to re-provision and pick up daughter Michelle and girlfriend Delsha, who joined us for a week of sailing.

Michelle's tips for visitors

Don't pack more than you can carry in a backpack. All you need is a swimsuit for daywear and a pair of shorts and T-shirt for evening. Shoes are optional. You'll need sun block, hat and sunglasses and personal items; also, saltwater-friendly shampoo, as you'll be showering in the ocean, although a fresh water rinse is available each day. Bring a camera and lots of film, as you won't believe your eyes. You can bring a book but you probably won't have time to read, although Sharon reads "bedtime" stories to guests. Be sure to do upper body workout, as you will need the strength for rowing and manning the sails. You will not be bored, as there are so many activities to keep you busy; such as, salsa making, snorkeling, spear-gun fishing, sea shell collecting and jewelry making. Spanish lessons and bargain shopping in Mexico will broaden your experience.

We had a great time aboard *Poet's Place*, with wonderful hosts, great food and entertainment... signed greenhorn deck-hands, Michelle and Delsha

Sharon
We are really glad we decided to see the Sea. The water is clear and filled with sea life. The days are hot, but we live in the water catching our dinner. We dine on seafood every night. We've met some fantastic people and have seen some unbelievable places. These are the good times. The most difficult time for me is the solitude, when for several days or weeks at a time, I don't see or talk to another human being other than Steve and contacts on VHF or ham radio. I really miss friends. Although I've met so many great people out here, we're always saying goodbye. E-mails mean a lot to us and we now have e-mail direct on the boat through the ham radio. When we get to San Carlos in late July to haul out to paint the bottom, we will be taking a bus into Phoenix to visit family and friends. We will then fly to Seattle for three weeks in August, to take care of some business.

Solitude

Sharon Reed-Hendricks

To sit and watch the sun come up
And greet a brand new day
To listen to the many sounds
Of morning on the bay

To hear the sound of seagulls cry
And smell the salty sea
To feel the warming of the sun
As it reaches out to me

To feel the wind upon my face
And taste the morning dew
And I shall set my sails today
For places far and new

To let the worries of the world
Just melt and pass me by
My early morning solitude
The sea, the wind and I

4 The Sea of Cortez

Sharon

To cruise Mexico and not see the Sea of Cortez would be missing a lot. The Sea of Cortez or the Golfo de California is a desert of stark beauty. At first you wonder what is here. Then you look close and its hidden beauty is breathtaking, both above and beneath the sea. The islands are colorful rock formations with caves, cactus, plants and white sand beaches where shells abound. Its many shades of turquoise water are so crystal clear you can see your anchor twenty-five feet below along with every pebble on the bottom. The warm daytime temperature reaches over 100 degrees in July-September, yet evenings are pleasant with a breeze and cooling to the 80's for sleeping. The water temperature during the spring and summer stays around 83-88 degrees. After snorkeling for a couple of hours, you actually feel cool. Snorkeling in the Sea with fish of every shape and color, colorful coral and underwater caves and canyons are stunning. It is truly an underwater wonderland to behold. We snorkeled and dove for our dinner and dined on fish, lobster, clams and scallops. Steve is becoming quite the diver and spear fisherman, and I, the gourmet seafood cook. While at anchor we dive and spear our fish, but while underway sailing, we catch most of our fish on a plastic squid lure dragged on top of the water about 120 feet behind us. We use a 200 pound test leader and 300 pound test line tied to a big rubber snubber (bungee shock cord to absorb the strike of a pound fish) to the boat. It helps to drag a Coke bottle or something twenty-five feet in front of the lure, as big game fish search the surface for any disturbance in the water and then they see the lure and grab it. We've lost count of the many dorado (mahimahi) we've caught.

We had five beautiful months in the Sea (May-October) excluding August when we flew back to Seattle for a visit. On most occasions, while sailing the Sea of Cortez, we saw whales, sea turtles, seals, giant manta rays and dolphins leaping in the air.

47

In May, after daughter Michelle's visit to La Paz, we headed north to the islands in the Baja's Sea of Cortez. There are twenty-nine islands here in the Sea and only two have permanent residents, so sailing the islands is remote. We were thankful for our water maker, a Pur 35 that makes one and a half gallons per hour. This is a super-fine membrane filter that takes the seawater and produces enough fresh water for our drinking, cooking and two showers a day (my necessary luxury).

We anchored in over thirty-five anchorages in the Sea of Cortez, all of which were beautiful and each so unique. It would fill several books to detail all of them, so we'll highlight the top ten or so. On Isla San Jose I thought I'd found shell nirvana. I collected so many different and beautiful shells I wasn't sure I'd get them all on the boat. I had to promise Steve I'd give most of them away. I didn't realize what a job that would be until we flew to Seattle. A backpack of shells weighs a ton!

In San Evaristo on the Baja, we walked over the hill to a village and its actively worked salt pans. Here I collected sea salt that we use every day in our salt grinder to season our food. Both Isla Monserrate and Aqua Verde were beautiful and the snorkeling was superb. We had the anchorage all to ourselves. Although I love the beauty of these remote anchorages, I find that after about four or five days I need to talk to someone other than Steve and the VHF radio. Steve, on the other hand could have stayed there for weeks. It had been over a week since we'd seen another boat and I was ready to move on. So we moved to Candeleros, not as pretty, but there was a retreat center on the beach, along with six other boats and friends. We had pot-luck dinners, a puppet show (I helped with this one), dancing and a jam session on the beach. We had so much fun we stayed for a week. Saying goodbye to all these people was difficult, as you never know when or where you'll meet again. The exciting part is the new friendships we formed and the possibility of meeting again out there, months or years down the way.

Our next stop was Puerto Escondido, a hidden harbor surrounded by hills and covered with desert scrub and cactus. It's lovely and filled with cruisers, even a permanent live-aboard population and a little yacht club building where potluck suppers, Sunday brunches and much more goes on. We did a repeat performance of the puppet show there for an audience of over 80 people. Needless to say, I was getting my people fill. It was while in Puerto Escondido that our friend Don Brown came to visit. Now Don and I have been celebrating our birthdays together for years by going out to lunch. I told Don that if he wanted to do lunch this year, he'd have to come to Mexico. So, come he did. Since Puerto Escondido is about a third of the way up the Baja and a little remote, this took some doing for Don to get to us. First he flew into Cabo where he lost his traveler's checks and then he took a bus to La Paz where he spent the night. The next morning he took another long bus ride (about five hours) to Loreto; getting off at the turnoff to Puerto Escondido and hitch-hiking a ride down to the anchorage where we picked him up by dinghy to deliver him to *Poet's Place* for lunch. Some people will do anything for a birthday lunch.

Don arrived with a small duffel bag and no snorkel gear. He said he didn't snorkel and didn't even swim. We handed him our extra snorkel gear and into the water he went. Once in, we thought we'd never get him out. We found him swimming laps around the boat early every morning. By the end of his visit, he was swimming like a fish. Don says next time he visits he will work out at a gym first. We had a great time snorkeling Isla Carmen with Don and sadly sailed him to Loreto for his bus trip back. Next year, we should be in Costa Rica for our birthdays. I have visions of Don swinging from the treetops with the monkeys making his way to the anchorage.

Working our way north up the sea, we stopped at Isla Coronados. It was a beautiful anchorage with clear blue water, so I decided to go snorkeling. I was just ready to jump in (Steve was down below) when I saw this huge black shark figure swimming toward the boat. In the background of my mind, I could hear the music to *Jaws*. I yelled for Steve and postponed my jump overboard. After it swam away, we figured out, with the help of another cruiser, that it was a whale shark. If only I had known that, I would have jumped in, as they are harmless, have no teeth and are rarely seen.

Each new anchorage held for us new surprises. When we dropped anchor in Punta Chivato, a voice came over our VHF radio, "Welcome to Punta Chivato". As I looked around (we were the only boat in the anchorage) I couldn't imagine where this voice was coming from. I got on the radio and asked, "Who are you and where are you?" "We're Jim and Mary," came an answer. "We are *Mooney Base*, and we're in the pink house on the beach. Cocktails are at our house at 5:30 p.m., please join us." I looked down the beach at a beautiful pink house with two people waving. What a welcome to this beautiful bay with white sandy beaches. *Mooney Base* was named after the Mooney airplane Jim flies and keeps in the hanger at their home on the beach. Jim and Mary are a warm friendly couple who welcome cruisers to their beautiful home. They have a book for visiting yachts to sign and are a wealth of information on the area and the people. We had a delightful time visiting with them, both on our way north and our way back south, enjoying lunch and potluck dinners with them. One day Mary and I walked to a shell beach to collect several varieties of seashells. On another day the four of us took a ride in their jeep to the town of Mulege, an oasis in the desert, complete with date palms. Through the desert scrub, a river flows from the mountains to the sea, forming a small delta. The town is shaded with flowering trees and a small town square. I bought some dates. They were by far the sweetest, most delicious dates I have ever eaten.

On our way south bound, we again stopped in Puma Chivato to visit with Jim and Mary. There were a couple of other boats at anchor with us so we had a few potluck dinners at their home. During one of these dinners, I was standing barefoot on the tile floor talking (that's what I do best) when this scorpion comes

50

out of nowhere, zaps my little pinkie toe with his stinger and runs under the counter. Talk about PAIN! It felt like a hot needle going through me. Unlike a bee sting, this pain repeats itself every ten seconds, shooting hot needle-like pain through my toe. Some of the people there had been stung before, so they knew to apply ice, elevate the foot, and take an antihistamine. There was a retired doctor living down the beach that took a look at it and said that it just takes time to heal. He also said that it's always worse for children and small adults. Great! I fit both categories. The pain lasted for about twenty-four hours and I felt the numbness for about a week.

San Sebastian was another beautiful little bay with a small community of about eighteen homes (mostly Americans). Everyone was super friendly, inviting us for dinner, giving us lobster and swapping stories about our adventures and life off the grid. This was such a beautiful *oasis in a desert* area, many miles from the nearest road. The little bay was just big enough to anchor two boats, was surrounded by unique homes of various designs and stages of development, all solar powered. It was fascinating to see the ingenuity people had used to pioneer this little waterfront settlement in such a remote but beautiful spot. It was on a 1,000 acre ranch property owned by a Mexican American and limited to twenty homes at that time. The owner loved this area so much when he was growing up; he immigrated to the U.S., built a successful carpet business, came back and bought the property he loved. The owner had made this his little paradise get away for his retirement. San Marcos Island is one of the two inhabited islands in the Sea of Cortez with an active Gypsum quarry at the south end. When we arrived I looked around this desolate island and wondered what was there. I suggested we leave for fear that the white gypsum powder would blow all over our decks. Steve insisted we stay and visit the village; it turned out to be one of our most memorable stops. This quaint little mining village is tucked behind a mountainside, with its brilliant white church cut from solid blocks of gypsum. We shopped at the well-stocked tienda (store) and started a conversation (in Spanish) with the manager.

We met another man, Agustin Casanova Cruz, who spoke perfect English. We found out he was the operations manager of the whole mining operation. He asked us if we'd like a tour of his gypsum mine and the island. Boy, would we! We were escorted into the company's new model air-conditioned truck and driven to Agustin's modern air-conditioned office where we were shown a video (in English) of the company's history and policy—all first class. There, we met Ofelia, a thirty-one-year-old female engineer who spoke fluent English. We were given hard hats to wear and off we went in the company truck for our all-day tour of the mining operation, the village and the island.

Steve

For 100 years San Marcos Island has been one of the world's main suppliers of gypsum used mainly for the manufacturing of wallboard, but also used in other products such as aspirin. The mine is an open pit type operation where they blast loose the gypsum rock with explosives then scoop up the rock with big front end loaders and dump it into huge off-road dump trucks. The trucks dump their load into a big hopper where the rock is crushed into baseball-sized chunks. At the bottom of the crusher, the rock drops onto a conveyer belt that runs for a mile and a half down to the dock where the ore is loaded onto big ships. Most of it is shipped to Georgia Pacific in the U.S., which owns forty-nine percent of the mine.

The mine employs about 150 people and with their families there are about 750 residents on the island. Many were born here and worked here all their life. But now there is only about ten to fifteen years of gypsum left to mine and then the town and the mine will turn into a ghost town, as there are no other resources on the island to sustain the community now owned by the mine.

Sharon

The village itself is lovely and well cared for by the company. Besides the church, there is a store, schools, a nice hospital and a well-lit baseball field. The company clubhouse is a modern facility with a pool and weight room, television and bar, all overlooking the water. Besides his home on the hill, Agustin Casanova also owns a big ranch complete with horses, cows, pigs, goats, and chickens; tended to by caretakers. We were invited to stay as long as we'd like as Agustin's guest and if there was anything we needed—just let him know. The hospitality was overwhelming! I guess not too many cruisers stop at this unique village, probably because of its remote location and desolation.

The north end of San Marcos is quite different, with superb snorkeling and diving. On a scale of 1 to 10 we'd give it a 15! There were several rock caves that one could swim or row the dinghy through. After traveling about fifty feet through one such cave, we came out at a small white sandy beach surrounded by bluffs. It was magical. The water was crystal clear and the sea life was abundant. We never went hungry or tired of seafood. We were planning to stay a day and ended up spending a week. One day while snorkeling and spear fishing on San Marcos, I dove to the "hidden beach." There was a group of young Mexican Navy guys on their day off gathered for a beach party, complete with music from a boom box. They invited us to join them and have some Ceviche (fish cooked in lime). They spoke no English but we managed fine with our limited Spanish. The Mexican Navy is supposed to enforce all the fishing rules, including spear fishing, which is supposedly prohibited on San Marcos. They borrowed Steve's snorkel and spear gun to spear some fish for the party. I guess it's not strictly enforced. We had a great afternoon and I even danced with one of the young officers.

By the middle of July we headed across the Sea of Cortez to San Carlos where we hauled the boat out of the water and into dry storage for a month. *Poet's Place* needed bottom paint (something you need to do every two to three years) and we needed a trip home, both to Arizona and Seattle. July in Mexico is hot (even for me), especially when the boat is out of the water. The boatyard was not fun and I missed the after-noon ocean breeze and diving overboard for a swim. We spent four days getting the boat ready to leave her for our trip home. Sails and equipment came down and were stored below. What couldn't come down was secured. Decks and cockpit were tarped and portholes secured and covered as this is hurricane season. It was quite a job and we were hot and bug bitten.

On July 21st we took a bus from San Carlos to Phoenix. These buses are first class with air-conditioning and movies. They are comfortable and inexpensive. But, this is Mexico, so our nine-hour trip took twelve hours. Although we didn't have to change buses, we did make several stops; some routine, some not. The bus driver had to get out and go under the bus to check something and got his white shirt all greasy, so we had to make a stop to get him a clean shirt. Then we stopped in the little village so the locals could get on to sell tacos. If everyone is hungry this can take a while. Then the driver got a stomach ache (too many tacos) and we got off the highway to find a store for some bright pink tablets. We also picked up his girlfriend who works at one of the bus stations and took her home—another off-the-highway stop. After that, it was customs at the border and then a broken down Mexican bus along the Arizona highway. Being the friendly, kind people Mexicans are, we had to stop and make room for all the stranded people along with the bus driver and take them to their stop. We're used to this, since we've lived in Mexico for a year now. We had a wonderful visit in Arizona, and then flew to Seattle visiting more friends than we knew we had. We tried to see everyone but missed some, so we decided we needed to visit every two years or so, if we could.

Even paradise has its price to pay. On the 31st of August we took a bus from Phoenix back to San Carlos and the real work began as we scraped, prepped and painted *Poet's Place* bottom ourselves. We've done this many times before, but never in one-hundred plus degree heat with matching humidity and bugs. The bugs would be so thick they would get into our eyes, our nose and my mouth (because it's always open). Those who envy our life style surely would not now. The saving grace was that we rented an air-conditioned motel with a kitchen so we could sleep and eat in comfort. For eight grueling days we worked from 5:00 a.m.-1:00 p.m., and then walked to the motel to eat and rest, then back to the boat yard by 5:00 p.m. to work until dark. We were very happy to get back into the water where boats and sailors belong. *Poet's Place* looked almost new again. We spent another week in San Carlos in the water getting things put back together. By mid-September we sailed across to the Baja side to start our journey south, retracing and revisiting many of our favorite anchorages and friends in the Sea of Cortez.

We will cross the Sea again in early November to mainland Mazatlan and then continue south to visit more of southern Mexico. We hope to be in Guatemala by April. We have been cruising for over a year now and realize that the cruising life is just that—it's cruising and its life. And like life, it has its ups and downs, its good days and bad. We love Mexico, but we're ready to see another country. I miss the people back home, but the desire to travel and visit other worlds keeps me going.

How much does it Cost to Cruise?

I think it's different for everyone. It depends on the people and the boat. It's like asking someone what it costs to live in Seattle. Everyone would have a different answer. We have always been very frugal, even back home. We don't stay at marinas; we anchor out (marinas in Mexico are expensive). We eat what the locals eat and eat out where they eat, not at the expensive tourist traps. We do eat out a lot. We fish for our meat, (stay away from red meat, it's healthier) and our drink of choice is water or limeade. We sailed most of the time, thus seldom turning on the engine and saving on fuel cost. Some call us purists. We do all our own maintenance and repair work. We kept pretty good track of our expenses and for the past year we have lived on less than $500 per month. This includes everything; food, eating out, fuel, boat parts, any medical needs, trips inland and fees. We allowed for $600, so we saved enough for a trip home. According to American standards, we are living under poverty level, yet somehow we feel very rich. We owe nothing to anyone, have no bills, eat well, feel healthy and are traveling the world. We wouldn't trade places with anyone.

Memories

Sharon Reed-Hendricks

Bittersweet memories
Of the days gone by
As I sit remembering
Then I start to cry

Thinking of all those times
Before I went away
Knowing that I had to go
Wishing I could stay

Memories are precious gifts
Tucked inside the heart
I take them out and bring them close
Whenever we're apart

The memories that we share
Are pictures of the past
Friends will come and friends will go
But memories will last

To always go where you must go
To be all that you can be
And learn to just let go and live
But keep the memory

58

ON

5 Mainland Mexico

Sharon

We had a bittersweet goodbye as we sailed across the *Sea of Cortez* and said farewell to the Baja and its crystal clear waters and abundant sea life. The good part was we got to visit all our favorite places on the mainland of Mexico that we sailed to last year, before deciding to turn around and see the Sea of Cortez for the summer. It was the end of October when we arrived once again in Mazatlan and had a busy two weeks re-visiting with friends, John and Sharon Townsell and our new friend Dora, in immigrations. We also stocked up with provisions for the arrival of daughter Michelle and boyfriend Leon who sailed with us for two weeks from Mazatlan to Puerto Vallarta and all the places in-between. Talk about getting to know your girlfriend's parents (and daughter's boyfriend). Two weeks in a small space with virtually no privacy is a good test. We must have all passed, as we had a great time and they say they are coming back.

Returning to the beautiful island of Isabela was twice as much fun for us with Michelle and Leon along. We had an overnight passage and arrived in the early morning sunrise to huge flocks of sea birds circling the island. Isabela is a magnificent bird sanctuary with numerous frigate birds nesting in the bushes with their fuzzy babies. Blue and yellow-footed boobies nest on the cliff tops, and terns and gulls live in trees surrounding the lake that is on the island. On shore, we hiked through the banana groves, sending Leon up the trees to pick fresh sun ripened bananas. We passed the Crater Lake and into the nesting grounds. The nests are in bushes, so we could get to within inches of them. Leon took several wonderful photos along the way, sometimes taking several minutes focusing to get the perfect shot. When we returned to the boat, he discovered that during all that picture taking he had no film in the camera.

We also did some fantastic snorkeling (Jacques Cousteau filmed here) around the island. This was Leon's first time snorkeling and he loved it. Steve speared some fish for dinner, and with a beautiful sunset, we had a perfect ending to a beautiful two-day visit to Isabela.

Our next stop was one of our favorite little towns - San Blas and its jungle estuary. Once again, it was even more fun the second time around with Michelle and Leon. In a Mexican panga we explored the jungle river; viewing crocodiles, turtles, fish and a variety of birds. The river is lined with thick jungle, draped with wild orchards cascading from the trees. We passed thatched huts on stilts surrounded by mangroves.

At the end of the river, in a beautiful setting surrounded by cliffs, flowers and foliage, is a crystal clear, spring-fed water pond, complete with Tarzan swing. Intriguing the child within, all four of us took turns swinging and jumping into the pond, while keeping a sharp eye on the two crocodiles on opposite ends of the pond. One of them wasn't too active, but the larger one on the far end decided to join in on the fun and moved too close for comfort - so we decided it was time to dry off and eat lunch. There was a little restaurant alongside of the pond where Leon treated us to a delicious seafood lunch. We all enjoyed San Blas and the bugs enjoyed us. If you happen to be on the beach around dusk (and we often were) it is feeding time for the bugs. They loved me, Michelle and Leon but not Steve. The three of us left San Blas looking like we had chickenpox; itching and applying ointment all the way to Las Tres Marietas.

Las Tres Marietas are three small islands in Banderas Bay, about twelve miles west of Puerto Vallarta. They are ignored by many cruisers and are one of Steve's favorite. The middle island, where we anchored, is inundated with caves to explore. Last time we were here on our way north, we enjoyed exploring these caves so much that we wanted to return. These limestone caves were carved millions of years ago by the ocean when the water level was much higher than it is now. Some of the caves obviously had inhabitants at one time. It was here, while anchored at the island, that Michelle got her sea life fix. We saw huge sea turtles, fish of every color, manta rays leaping out of the water, whales breaching and dolphins came to play every morning. In addition, delightful surprises awaited us below as we snorkeled the islands' beautiful waters. Steve (the great tanned hunter) again speared some delicious fish for our dinner. This was a perfect way to end a perfect day.

Time was passing all too quickly and Michelle and Leon's two weeks deluxe cruise was almost over. It was time to head the boat to La Cruz, another of our favorite little towns, untouched by tourism and only ten miles north of Puerto Vallarta, where our guests would fly back to the wet-lands of Washington. La Cruz, with its cobblestone streets had everything we need and at a much lower price than Puerto Vallarta. Leon insisted on taking us out for dinner (he needed to use up some pesos) and was shocked when the total bill for chicken dinner for all four, including drinks, came to $6.50. We just couldn't spend all his pesos, so I guess he'll have to come back.

While in Mexico, Leon got addicted to the fruit bars. Unlike popsicles or fruit bars in the states, the ones in Mexico have real chunks of fruit in them and are usually homemade, all for the cost of forty cents. By the time he left La Cruz, Leon had cleaned out the ice cream store of their lime fruit bars. The day before Thanksgiving, with tears in our eyes, we bid farewell to Michelle and Leon—they announced they had such a good time that they would be back in six months for three weeks, because two wasn't long enough. Then I really cried. Some kids just keep coming home. Thanksgiving Day was spent at our favorite chicken place in La Cruz, shared with our Canadian cruising friends from S/V *Shadowfax*.

More company for *Poet's Place* B&B (boat and breakfast). We had only a week to wait, while we caught up with boat repairs, for our next set of company to arrive. Pat and Barry Conger from Seattle arrived December 1st for a week of sailing to Las Tres Marietas (island of the caves) and sightseeing La Cruz and Puerto Vallarta. Pat snorkeled for the first time and really enjoyed it. Barry twisted his ankle upon arrival on the island, so he got to relax more than he intended. Barry is a dentist and I talked him into bringing his dental tools and setting up practice under the palapa on the beach to check my teeth. It was good to learn that my three new crowns, by a Mexican lady dentist in San Carlos, looked really good. Barry said she did a great job. I paid $350 for all three crowns and Barry said it would have cost $2500 in his office. I couldn't afford to live in the States anymore.

During their short stay, we talked Dr. Barry into doing the local radio net that I do once a week. He did such a great job that he is now thinking about a new career (still working with the mouth). Seems Barry didn't really want to visit Mexico, but came at Pat's request. Pat says he now wants to make it an annual event. I guess Mexico worked its charm on Barry.

Cruising is always saying goodbye and we said our goodbyes to Pat and Barry and to La Cruz. We headed south to Isla Colorado near Chamela, where we anchored in crystal clear water and were joined by our friends on *Shadowfax*. This was to be the last time we would share an anchorage with them (at least for a very long time) as they were heading west to the South Pacific and we were headed south to Guatemala. We shared some potluck dinners and some fantastic snorkeling. This is where I watched in awe as a huge manta ray swam beneath me in all its splendor just a few feet away.

We sailed on to Tenacatita, a beautiful and tranquil anchorage with a white sand beach and swaying palms, just like the movies. In fact, the little French restaurant on the beach is where they filmed the movie *McHale's Navy*. There is no town here, just a beautiful tropical beach with a palapa restaurant and a jungle river to dinghy up. Every morning and evening, the dolphins came to play between the boats in the anchorage. At the other end of the bay, I noticed other cruisers in the water with the dolphins one morning, so I swam over to investigate. It seemed the dolphins did indeed swim with the people. The very next day, December 16th, was a day to remember. Two dolphins came early to the anchorage and I dove into the water as they swam near the boat. Steve got into the dinghy and followed, directing me to them. They were in a playful mood. I had on my facemask so I could see under the water. Within minutes they were swimming underneath me and beside me, close enough to touch. It was the thrill of a lifetime and a dream come true—swimming with the dolphins in the wild. It was my early Christmas present.

Continuing south, we spend Christmas anchored in the lagoon at Barra de Navidad with about ten other cruising boats. Barra de Navidad is a charming little town with lush tropical hillsides surrounding the lagoon. There was a little church on the hillside, and at night during the week of Christmas, we could hear the church bells ringing and the lovely singing drifting across the anchorage—a perfect setting for the season. It did seem strange having 80 degree weather for Christmas. On Christmas Eve under the shade of a palapa, we had a pot-luck on the beach of a little island in the lagoon with about forty other cruisers and locals. We had a white elephant gift exchange, great food, Christmas music and terrific weather. This is my kind of holiday—low stress. However, the difficult part was that we really missed our family, especially grandkids and friends.

After Christmas, we again headed south for a two-day, two-night passage to Zihuatanejo (better known as Z-town). We stopped at Punta Carrizal (beautiful remote anchorage) around the corner from Manzanillo and Isla Granda (close to Z-town). We arrived in Z-town on New Year's Eve to a display of fireworks over the entire bay. It took us a few days to catch up on our sleep and start to explore the town. Z-town seems to be a favorite hangout for cruisers, many staying for months each season. We liked it, but not as much as some. A little too touristy for us, but it is a beautiful setting with the town set into the lush green hills surrounding the bay. We waited here to meet Steve's sister Sherry and husband Jerry, who have come to vacation here the last two years. They were delivering our mail, along with other hard to find items from the States. It was great to visit with family and we were able to anchor right in front of their hotel.

While in Z-town, I decided to see why I hadn't been feeling my usual energetic self for the past several months; I decided to visit a doctor. I had nausea, (and I don't get seasick) headaches and no energy off and on for a few months. This decision came about after a good cruising friend of ours died just a few months before and his wife returned to Z-town to scatter his ashes in the bay (Z-town was his favorite place). Several cruisers took dinghies to the middle of the bay to join in this sad but fitting farewell to our friend. I was scared to go to the doctor, as I didn't want to be the next set of ashes. The doctor had been highly recommended by another cruising friend who had been a patient there a few years before. They are now personal friends of the doctor and his wife and they accompanied me to the clinic/hospital where I was put through several tests, ultrasounds, blood test, etc. I had the results the same afternoon. Salmonella poisoning, good news compared to what it could have been. I didn't have to wait for an okay from my insurance company or primary care physician (since we have neither). Total cost for all tests, medications and doctor was $150.00. Not much more than the co-pay for doctor, lab and X-rays back home. We were all surprised that I wasn't sicker than I was. Then the doctor invited us all to his home to have lunch with him and his wife. Steve says it was the best meal he ever had in Mexico. We were also given a bag of fresh grapefruit from his ranch and his wife gave me some special tea for my stomach. This would never happen in the States. Even going to the doctor can be an adventure in Mexico.

A few days later Steve's brother-in-law Jerry twisted his foot while walking through town. We told him no problem, we know this doctor around the corner. So back we went to the hospital where the nurses had a good laugh at his size thirteen foot (they don't see them this size in Mexico). After x-rays it was determined he only sprained it. They wrapped his big foot in an ace bandage, applied ice and he was ordered to stay off it for a couple of days.

Needless to say, our most frequently visited place in Z-town was the hospital/clinic. We hated to say goodbye to our family, all our cruising friends and new friends we had made at the hospital, but it was time to head south to Acapulco where our next set of company was to meet us.

Acapulco was a nice surprise, with much of its city built on the hillsides overlooking the spectacular bays. The tropical lushness of flowers and birds of the surrounding hillside are breathtakingly beautiful. The city of Acapulco itself is big and noisy and reminds me of downtown Los Angeles, but the surrounding hills and towns are lovely. We anchored in the lovely little bay of Puerto Marques, around the corner from Acapulco Bay, where the quaint little town behind the palapas had everything we needed. For larger provisioning we took the local bus, for 3.5 pesos into Acapulco. The bus ride is the best deal in town, as it takes you along the coast and up the hillside with spectacular views of the bays below.

Sharon sells seashells and/or laundry
While in Marques, we needed to do some laundry and figured I had too much to do by hand. I was told there was no laundry facility in town and should go to Acapulco. Being the independent person I am and always looking for a challenge, I decided that I would find someone in town who wouldn't mind doing some extra laundry for some extra pesos. I was confident that my Spanish was good enough to get this across. We walked through the town, Steve and I each carrying a large bag of laundry, asking several women if they do laundry. All of them said "No" until finally one said "*Si*" and led us into her humble home. I guess I didn't ask enough

65

questions, as she seemed anxious to have the job. She looked the laundry over with great care as I asked how much it would be. I thought it was strange when she asked me how much, but I figured she wasn't in the laundry business and didn't know what was a fair price. When my first price was too high, she suggested fifty pesos ($5.00), which to my delight, was the best price I ever paid for so much laundry.

We talked about everything (in Spanish); her son's wedding, her new grand baby and then I said I'd see her tomorrow, which is when she said to come back. The next day, as Steve and I sat at her kitchen table, she handed me fifty pesos! I looked at Steve in surprise as he said, "I think you just sold our clothes." The blood drained from my face as I asked where our clothes were. I had visions of all the Mexican neighbors walking around town with our clothes on, not to mention sleeping on our only two sets of sheets, and we had company coming in a few days. Finally after much explaining, in Spanish and sign language, she went into the other room and returned with our laundry. The color had returned to my face and we both laughed at our mistake. She said she would wash the clothes, not sell them, for fifty pesos (at this point I think she felt sorry for me) and they would be ready by 4:00 p.m. Sure enough, we had sparkling clean clothes that I now know are worth only fifty pesos.

After a few days in Acapulco, Rick and Roxanna Bryant of Portland Oregon, who stayed aboard our luxury yacht for a week, joined us (more mail and goodies from the states). While they were here, we sailed over to watch the cliff divers from the comfort of our home. It was something I always wanted to see and I can now say I've seen them from the bow of our own boat, it was awesome. We also sailed over to Isla Roqueta (around the corner from Acapulco Bay) to spend a day. While at the island, we spotted a shrimp boat at anchor. Roxanna had been hungry for shrimp ever since she arrived. Everyone decided that I should be the one to go negotiate as I knew more Spanish and was a good barterer. I told them that was debatable, as I almost sold our clothes, but they sent me anyway. Rick rowed the boat and I did the talking. Rick had brought us some trading items, so off we went with our bag of goodies. We did good. For three baseball caps, a calculator and two magazines, we got a big bag of jumbo shrimp and two huge lobsters. Rick was sure it was the calculator, but I thought it was the magazine; I had turned to the page with the sexy girl falling out of her bathing suit top. Steve says it was the purple bathing suit I wore. We may never know, but the dinner was superb.

Steve

After we said our farewells to Rick, Roxanna and Acapulco, we had a three-day, three- night sail to Huatulco. Late afternoon about seventy miles south of Acapulco, I had just made a sail change when I went forward to sort out some of the lines and halyards laying at the base of the mast. As I grabbed a hand full of rope and pulled it out from under the storm sail bag, I saw a rope I didn't recognize. I couldn't believe my eyes. Holy cow, it was moving. It was then I realized that's not a rope, it's a snake. A big snake! I was yelling at Sharon, "There's a big snake on our boat, get me the boat hook and get the camera!" With the boat hook holding his head down, I managed to untangle him from the rest of the lines as he twisted around everything. I moved him to a clear spot on the deck where we could get a good look at him. He was about six feet long with markings similar to a rattlesnake. We took a picture of him and pitched him overboard. We don't know how he got onboard, but our best guess is he climbed up our self-steering gear at one of the anchorages during the past few weeks. He could have been onboard a month or more, as I had not moved that sail bag for a while. We still don't know what kind of a snake it was, or if it was poisonous or not. But we have a good photo so we will see if someone can identify it. Just another one of those strange things that happen out here that make this sailing life interesting. Later we identified it as a boa constrictor that was rather thin from living on our deck not finding anything to eat there.

Sharon

At a stop in Puerto Angel, fifteen miles north of Huatulco, we were hailed and boarded by the Mexican Navy and their adorable black lab drug sniffing dog. Everyone was very friendly, especially the dog who wanted me to keep petting her. They checked everything and everywhere. When they checked the bilge and found Steve's hidden bottle of pickled quail eggs, they thought that was the funniest thing they ever saw and had to show it to all the other guys waiting on the deck with their machine guns. After a good laugh and eating a couple dozen cookies and asking the usual questions, they left. I still have black dog hairs all over my white decks. We also stopped in several little bays around the corner from Huatulco. In one particular little bay, hidden between two reefs, surrounded by white beaches and crystal clear water with room for only one boat to anchor, was our own private little paradise. On the beach were two chairs under a tree (just like they were waiting for us). We stayed several days for some fantastic snorkeling and beachcombing (and sitting in the chairs provided). Now we are waiting in Huatulco for a good weather window to cross the dreaded Tehuantepecs, a 250-mile area leading into Guatemala.

Steve
The Tehuantepecs can be described in one word—*windy*. This gulf is adjacent to the Isthmus which is a huge north-south valley running across the narrowest section of Mexico, between two massive mountain ranges. The winds sweeping over the Isthmus maintain a yearly average of 25 knots and are often 35 to 40 knots. Since these are off shore winds we have to sail very close to shore just outside the breakers to avoid the high steep seas that build just a little farther out. This takes maximum concentration watching charts, depth sounder and radar, especially at night. We will be glad to have the Tehuantepecs behind us.

After eighteen months cruising Mexico, it's sad to say goodbye, but we're excited to see Central America. New adventures await us.

The Rest of Your Life

Sharon Reed-Hendricks

May the rest of your life
Be filled with love and joy
May that love spread itself
To every girl and boy

May your fondest wish come true
And you know its worth
May your dream of happiness
Spread across this earth

May you find an inner peace
Inside of every man
And find a way that it can spread
Itself across the land

May you feel the warmest glow
Fill your heart's desire
May it spread throughout the world
Setting it on fire

May you always greet someone
With arms open wide
May you open up your heart
And let the world inside

6 Central America and Costa Rica to Panama

Sharon

It's hard to believe we've been gone two years. Since leaving our Marina in Everett, Washington, we have traveled over 7,000 nautical miles and visited seven countries. At this rate I figure we'll be in our nineties by the time we reach Africa.

We safely made the three day dreaded Tehuantepec crossing (250 mile area between Mexico and Guatemala). The first day and night were the most difficult with thirty-five knot winds, but flat seas. We made a brief stop in Puerto Medero to rest overnight before saying farewell to Mexico and heading for Guatemala.

The *Forgotten Middle* refers to the Central American countries of Guatemala, El Salvador, Honduras and Nicaragua that are often missed by travelers and cruisers on their way to Costa Rica, Panama or the South Pacific. Before visiting these countries, I knew and heard very little about them. They are little diamonds in the rough and should not be missed if heading this way. They truly are unforgettable.

I cannot begin to tell you how incredibly beautiful, colorful, and inexpensive Guatemala is. We truly fell under its spell. We traveled by bus inland for about a week (this was not long enough). It was a trip of spectacular mountain scenery. The natives still wear their traditional colorful outfits. One can see the women and little girls in long skirts and hand-embroidered tops all carrying fresh fruits, veggies or laundry balanced on their heads and wrapped in colorful cloths. The men wear colorful tops, hats and pants with a kilt-type cloth wrapped around their waist and they carry hand-woven purses. Women carry babies wrapped in brightly colored cloth slung around their back or front while balancing fruits on their heads. It was incredible, like stepping back in time, or being

71

in another world.

The hillsides are farmed in terraces and the scenery is one of green lushness. Everything is done by hand, no machines. The air was cool and clear in the mountains. Palm trees, tropical flowers and pine trees were everywhere. It was the best of two worlds; tropical and mountainous landscapes. We traveled by chicken bus to Antigua, a charming old world city that time forgot and progress ignored. The one and two-story buildings, cobbled streets and colonial squares nestled in the mountains make this a must see place. We plan to return someday and stay, perhaps for several months, but who knows when. We stayed at a charming, Spanish-style hotel with our own bathroom for $10.00 per night. Food was very cheap, as was everything else.

From Antigua, we traveled higher into the mountains to Lake Atitlan; a beautiful huge lake in a valley surrounded by volcanoes. We traveled with another cruising couple, but they took the expensive direct bus and Steve and I took the extremely cheap chicken bus driven by the driver from hell. It was a hoot. Actually it took four buses to get there, but that was part of the fun. We then took a local panga across the lake to a little village, where once again, we saw natives in colorful dress balancing everything and anything on their heads. One girl let me try the head balance. This is not easy as my head is not as flat as theirs and I dropped everything.

Guatemalan buses are extremely colorful and crowded. The driver and his assistant try to pack as many passengers and chickens as possible into their bus. The profit motive appears to be alive and well. Buses designed for forty-five people are packed with ninety passengers. They place three to a seat designed for two making the aisle nonexistent. Being old, crippled or carrying three babies does nothing to get you a seat. It's first come, first to grab a seat. The driver's assistant is most entertaining as he somehow makes his way from the front of the bus, between the packed bodies, all the way to the rear; collecting fares and giving change, then going out the window in the rear to climb onto the roof of the bus. He then comes down the side using the forward window as a step to enter the front of the bus again. All this is done while the bus is moving along at record-breaking speeds through the narrow winding roads and heavy traffic.

A two day, two night passage brought us to the Bay of Jiquilisco, El Salvador. After radio contact, we were met by a panga who led us through the breakers across the river bar and guided us for two hours up the river to Barillas. We heard about Barillas Marina Club via other cruisers and decided it was a good place to do some inland travel in El Salvador. For $5US per day, Barillas Marina Club offer mooring balls to tie the boat up to. We also had the use of their swimming pool, clubhouse, laundry, showers and an air-conditioned van ride into town to shop. At that time, thirty other cruising boats moored at the jungle estuary river. Needless to say, the clubhouse was busy with potlucks, movie night, jam sessions and get-togethers. About a month before we arrived, an earthquake that devastated several of the near-by towns and villages hit El Salvador. The cruisers at Barillas adopted one of the villages in the mountains and we were part of the group that pitched in to help re-build the village. This was a great opportunity to witness firsthand the effects of the quake and the mountain village life of the coffee plantations of El Salvador.

While at Barillas, we took a jungle walk to visit the spider monkeys that live in the mango trees. It was my first time to see monkeys in the wild—what a thrill. They ate bananas right out of our hands, provided they were not too ripe (these monkeys were particular). We had so much fun with the monkeys it was hard to leave.

On a sad note, one of the boats that left Barillas a few days before us to sail to Costa Rica caught fire, burned, and sank. Luckily, two other cruising boats were in the area and saw the fire (at night). They were able to rescue the single-handler, who was badly burnt. Several of us cruisers, including a cruiser doctor in Barillas were part of the rescue via radio. We were up half the night listening to the radio as the drama unfolded. On the radio the doctor asked the lady on the rescue boat if they had any morphine in their medical kit. She said "Yes" but she had never given a shot before. The doctor walked her through the process as we all felt the pain of the needle as she injected it. Later that night we helped pass messages to the El Salvador Navy and coordinate their interception of the rescue boat. The Navy then took the injured skipper to the hospital. We never really found out what caused this fire but it sounded suspicious and rumors were that maybe the owner was behind on boat payments and torched the boat for insurance money. Hard to prove, especially in El Salvador.

While in El Salvador, we made friends with Antonio, a young local man, working in the office at Barillas. I expressed to him my desire to learn more Spanish. I asked him if he knew of any Spanish language schools where I could live and study Spanish for a week or so. To my surprise, the next day he excitedly announced that Steve and I would be most welcome to stay with his family. He explained that no one in his family spoke English but him and since he was at work all day, it would be a good opportunity to learn Spanish. I wasn't sure what I was getting into, but I'm always ready for an adventure. The next day Antonio's cousin, who also works at Barillas, drove us to the village; through the scenic farmland, passing ox carts and women carrying laundry on their heads. It was as if he were driving us back in time.

Antonio's family welcomed us with open arms. His sister Daisy (yes, Daisy) and sister Blanca became my personal teachers, while his father Juan made Steve his farmhand. Maria, Antonio's mother, did her best to teach me how to make tortillas and other El Salvadoran dishes. Their modest farmhouse has a dirt floor, where the chickens come and go as often as the people. It was very clean. The chickens were fed corn in the house and that took care of the bugs, as the chickens ate the bugs. There was an outhouse for your personal needs and an outdoor three sided brick shower with cold water from a well that was pumped into a bucket and dumped over your body after you soap up. It really felt good considering it was 90 degrees outside. Laundry was carried on Blanca's head down to the river to be washed on the rocks and rinsed in the clear flowing water, then carried home to hang on the line to dry. These girls have great posture!

The day started early at 5:00 a.m. with the sound of hands clapping to form the homemade tortillas. Blanca and Daisy milked the cows while their father saddled up the horses. They walked the cows about two miles to a pasture where they grazed and drank from the river until dusk. Everyone works hard, yet they rest and play a lot too. They have no car, no refrigerator, no washer or dryer and only a small black and white TV on which they watch the evening news. Their main mode of transportation is still a wooden wheel ox cart. Their house was made of adobe (sun-dried mud bricks) with a dirt floor. It's a simple, good life and everyone seems so happy and loving. Neighbors help neighbors. It must have been how it was a hundred years ago in the States. Have we really progressed that much with all our stress, pollution and unhappy people? Maybe we should learn from them.

One of the most interesting fruits in El Salvador was the Maranon fruit that grows on trees everywhere. Antonio's farm was full of them, along with bananas, mangos and citrus. The Maranon has the cashew nut, which hangs off the bottom of the yellow-orange, pear-like fruit. They first dry the hard shell in the sun for several days. Once dried, it's thrown into an open fire till it is charred, then cracked open with a hammer, removing the nut and then roasting it one more time on a flat pan over an open fire. A lot of work when there is only one nut on each fruit. No wonder cashews are so expensive. Boy do they taste good when they are this fresh. When we left Antonio's family we were all crying and we promised to return someday. The morning we left Barillas, Antonio sent a panga driver out to our boat to bring us a gift from his family. It was a big bag of cashews. I cried again. We will never forget this generous family and our wonderful memories of El Salvador.

Steve

For years El Salvador was a country of poor people dominated by a
few wealthy families, who owned all the land and manipulated
the government and military to control the general population to
work almost like slaves in the coffee and sugar cane fields.
In the 70's, the people rebelled and there was a terrible civil
war. The wealthy controlled the military and the police, plus they
had tremendous financial and military backing from the U.S. government. My question is why does our U.S. government get involved supporting this kind of government? (The same thing happened in Nicaragua and Colombia) Why?

The civil war ended in 1992 with the government agreeing to re-
distribute some of the land. Now ordinary people can own land
again and the country is beginning to develop once more. But the
poor are poorly educated and the wealthy seem to like it that way
(education beyond grade school is not free). Even though the re-
bels won the war, they had few people educated enough to take
over the government. So once again the wealthy families control
the government and are beginning to buy back their land.

Sharon

From El Salvador we sailed to the Gulf of Fonseca, which El Salvador, Honduras and Nicaragua all share, as all three countries
come together in this bay. We visited several of the islands in the
bay, enjoying swimming, fishing and visiting the little villages.

It always blows like hell off the coast of Nicaragua. It's great for
sailing, but hard on the nerves. We stopped a few places to rest for
the night along this coast. By the time we neared San Juan Del
Sur, we decided to pull into a beautiful little bay, one mile
around the corner from Del Sur to wait out the blow. It blew 30 to
40 knots for eight days straight. The seas in the anchorage were so
big we couldn't put the dinghy in the water to get to shore. The
current was so bad we couldn't swim.

So there we were, stuck on the boat with only each other. Talk about testing the relationship. Thank God for the radio net each morning where I could complain to all the other cruisers about my situation. I did a lot of writing and baking. I think both of us gained ten pounds. Finally, by day eight the wind slacked down to thirty. We decided we had better sail around the corner or we may be stuck here forever (or until one of us kills the other).

San Juan Del Sur was a wonderful surprise. It was a lovely town with Caribbean style buildings and very inexpensive. We could eat a meal, including drinks, for three dollars total for the two of us. We loved this place; the wind always blows, keeping things cool. I talked with everyone and anyone, as I needed my people fix after eight days on the boat. We really enjoyed the super nice Port Captain here.

For a donation, a water taxi would pick us up at our boat and take us to the pier. It was a hoot. Like something out of a junkyard. It was a panga of sorts with a doghouse built on top and about fifty tires tied all around the outside for bumpers. You entered on the roof, descended down the steep prong ladder to stand among the fish and fishermen. Often, several assorted men were hanging off the roof and the sides of the boat. I was usually the only female aboard, but hey, it got me to town. While in Del Sur we visited an ex-cruiser who was building a beautiful hotel there. We had great fun with the spider monkey that lives on his property. This monkey only liked men and fell in love with Steve. He climbed all over him giving him kisses and hugs. He would have nothing to do with me.

A few days before Easter, we dropped the hook in Santa Elena and raised our Costa Rican flag. It was good to be in Costa Rica. Santa Dena is a beautiful protected bay with magnificent scenery and untouched solitude. Howler monkeys surrounded this place; they wake you at 5:00 a.m. along with the parrots.

We had Easter dinner with four other cruisers in the cockpit of the largest boat (not ours). We then sailed to Playa Panama Costa

Rica, where a young Tico (that's what Costa Rica calls their locals) couple runs a very cruiser-friendly palapa restaurant on the beach with good food. The pretty wife gives salsa dance lessons to cruisers. At the time, there were about twelve other boats in the anchorage. We had many potlucks, salsa dance classes and great memories. It was sad to see the boats leaving, since many were on a fast track to get through the Panama Canal and others to the Galapagos and South Pacific. Next year we will head to the Galapagos, because we took our time and tried to see everything.

After anchoring in several more bays heading south, we entered the Golfo De Nicoya. What a gem. I had no idea the islands in this Gulf were so beautiful. It reminded me of sailing the San Juan Islands of Washington State, but more tropical. We had flat calm seas and plenty of wind, which made sailing these islands really fun. Just inside the Gulf, Bahia Ballena was a great place to visit. We took a day trip with another cruising couple to Montezuma; a cute, funky little village, reminding me of the 60's hippie days. We then took a hike to a beautiful waterfall and swam in the pool beneath it.

Islas Tortugas was a picture-perfect postcard setting; complete with a beautiful white sand beach, swaying palm trees, turquoise water and colorful parrots everywhere. They bring tourist over via boat about 10:00 a.m. and they are gone by 3:00 p.m. This is the slow season so there weren't very many tourists. We got to know the staff on this island pretty well and somehow they talked us into trying the canopy ride. Canopy rides are very popular in Costa Rica. In the forest there is a series of platforms about one-hundred feet up in the trees. You first hike up a mountainside to the first platform where they harness you to a rope and you rapidly descend down the rope to the second platform. After you catch your breath, you leap off the platform to the next platform, like a monkey jumping from tree to tree. I guess the idea is to view the forest from way up high like the monkeys, but it scares all the animals in the forest as you go screaming down this rope. It scared the crap out of me. Steve loved it. When they harnessed and clipped me to the first rope and I looked down from way up there, I thought I would die. I told everyone I couldn't do it. I wanted out of the harness and wanted to go back. While I was talking they clipped me on to the rope, sending me screaming down through the forest. I yelled, "Oh shit" all the way down. It's kind of like bungee jumping only you don't come back up. The only reason I went in the first place was because they offered us a special. If two go, the third one is free - I was the freebie and it was only $10US for Steve. The other cruiser guy that went with us was seventy-four years old and loved it.

Before we departed this island, the staff rowed out to our boat and gave us a big bag of mangos. Costa Rica is the land of monkeys and mangos—they are everywhere. We just walk down the road and pick mangos off the ground where they fall or the locals are always giving us bags of mangos. Being in Costa Rica is like being in a zoo, only instead of watching the animals, they watch you. I'd be walking down the road and feel something drop on my head. When I looked up, it was a monkey dropping a mango. Horses and cows wander the road and stop to stare. The lizards and iguanas are everywhere. Parrots, macaws and toucans are seen on a regular basis. Parakeets poop all over our boat and it's a mess, but I love seeing and hearing them. There are so many islands and so many stories to tell.

We left our boat at anchor for a week of inland travel at Playa Naranjo, where I learned to mimic the howler monkeys. We visited a friend of ours from Washington who lives outside of San Jose, high in the mountains. We saw some of the most spectacular scenery we have ever seen. It's hard to describe in words or pictures what we were privileged to view. Our friend Lynn took us to places where I'm sure no tourist and few Tico's ever go. We had a great visit.

It is now the rainy season in Costa Rica and I couldn't believe I was there. This is why I left Seattle. Actually, it's very different than Seattle. For one thing, it's warmer and usually it's sunny in the morning, then it clouds up around twelve o'clock noon and by 5:00 p.m. it downpours. The good part is that it cools things down to the 70's and washes off the boat and we don't have to use our water maker. The bad part is the rain is here until November.

On the afternoon of June 9th, while anchored at Punta Leona (a luxury resort that allows cruisers to use all their facilities free) *Poet's Place* was hit by lightning. We took a direct hit to our mast. The other cruisers in the anchorage saw smoke coming out of the mast. We had sparks flying inside the boat. I guess we are lucky to be alive, and our damage was minimal, although it was bad enough. We lost both our depth finders, several lights, a couple of radios (not our ham radio or computer, thank God) and our engine ignition .Our whip antenna on top of the mast exploded at the base and fell to the deck, melted and bent like a coat hanger. Needless to say, our stay here was longer than intended. The other cruisers were a wonderful help tracking down replacement parts. It took Steve two weeks to repair most of the damage. It's times like this that I wonder if I want to keep cruising. In El Salvador our refrigerator and toilet both went the same day. There is always something breaking down on a boat and though Steve can fix anything, it is very difficult to get parts in these countries since they don't usually carry them. It is not like the U.S. where you can just call and order. There is also Customs, which charge stiff taxes, and in Costa Rica it's eighty percent. Everything is more expensive in Costa Rica. Thanks to the cruising community and e-mail, we were able to contact a cruising friend visiting the States and he delivered the needed parts to us when he returned to Costa Rica a week later.

Last night we sat in the cockpit eating jumbo garlic shrimp (we traded a shrimp boat two baseball caps for a big bucket of shrimp), listening to soft music and watching the crimson sunset silhouetting the palm trees on the beach. Today two scarlet macaws flew over my head and played in the tree while I watched in awe. I think I'll keep cruising. We are now on our way to Panama, where we will spend about six months exploring the many islands. When we reach the Panama Canal we have a tough decision to make—turn right and head for the South Pacific, or turn left and head for the Caribbean. Both are equally enticing.

There's A Time and There's A Season

Sharon Reed-Hendricks

There's a time and there's a season
And a place for everything
There's a purpose and a reason
Like when winter turns to spring

There's a time for new beginnings
And a time to say good-bye
There's a time for loss and winning
To let go and then to cry

There's a time when we need laughter
And a time when we need tears
And there is a morning after
When the night is full of fears

There's a time to be a child
Time to run and time to play
There's a time just to be wild
Spread your wings and fly away

There's a time to stay and ponder
And a time when we need change
There's a time for us to wander
And to move and rearrange

There's a time we need to worry
And a time to just let go
There's a time for us to hurry
When we'd rather just be slow

There's a time and there's a season
Time to live and time to die
There's a purpose and a reason
We can't feel unless we cry

82

7   Panama and the Canal

Sharon

All is not perfect in Paradise. Since the lightning strike in Costa Rica, *Poet's Place* has had a series of events that had us questioning our direction with the boat and with life. Before leaving Costa Rica, I decided to go to San Jose for a routine mammogram. They found a cyst, one I had before, that had grown and changed in thickness. I needed a biopsy, so I stayed to have it done. It was benign—so that was good news, but it was a worry and an expense we did not expect (still less than U.S.)

In July, while traveling in remote areas of Panama, our computer crashed and we lost communication with everyone. It was three months until we finally got a new computer (that's another story). We still had ham radio communications and did some phone patches back to family to let them know what had happened, but it was awful. I had not realized how much I depend on the computer for my connection with friends and family back home. My mother had a stroke during this time and I worried about her condition. Being without a computer was very difficult for us.

When we were in Panama City (civilization), I went to the dermatologist to have a couple of dark moles checked. I had had malignant melanoma twice, once five years ago and another four years ago, so I am at high risk for skin cancer. The biopsy revealed another malignant melanoma on my back in the same area of the other two. The dermatologist sent me to an oncologist who suggested surgery. So it was back to the hospital. The hospital in Panama was a large, beautiful, modern facility. I had two nurses, one who assisted the doctor and one that massaged me through the entire procedure. The doctor bill was $200 for the surgery and the hospital bill was $150. Panama uses U.S. currency. It was the best hospital experience I have ever had.

Luckily we are catching the melanomas in the very early stages before they metastasize. Steve can find one better than the doctors as he notices the slightest change and then insists I get it removed. He has saved my life more than once. We had a long talk with the doctor, who was trained in Boston and New York, about continuing cruising. He said we should live our dream and continue to get the moles removed as we note changes and to wear protection when in the sun. He said I could live in an igloo in Alaska and still have this problem. It is still scary stuff and was a setback emotionally and financially. I am really getting to know the doctors and the medical facilities in Central America and I cannot say enough good about the quality of care I have received here. Such are the challenges of life, whether living on land or sea. For me, it's friends that help get me through. The cruising community has been so caring and supportive which really helps when we are so far away from family and friends. Enough about the challenges of life and on to the adventure.

Panama—it's more than just a canal
We arrived at Isla Parida Panama on the 4th of July, early in the morning after a two-day, two-night sail from Golfito Costa Rica. Our friends on sailing vessel *Vite* paddled out to greet us in their kayaks, as they were the only other boat anchored off this pristine island. It looked as if we had arrived in the South Seas with white sand beach, thick jungle and clear water. We were fascinated to watch a man with an old single bit ax on the beach transforming an old log into a beautiful twenty-foot dugout canoe. Each day we came to check on his progress and he proudly showed us how it was done. It took him seven days of steady chipping, using methods passed on from father to son for many generations. The final product was a work of art with graceful lines. The canoes are the main mode of transportation in this part of Panama. The man's sons came out to our boat daily to trade for lobster and fruit. Every night our friends on *Vite* and us dined on fish that we speared, lobster or shrimp.

One morning, Steve and I decided to take a hike through the jungle to the other side of the island. Filo (the local man) showed us the path and lent us his machete to help clear the way. It was like being in a *Tarzan* movie. After blazing our way through the jungle of banana trees, orchards draping from air plants in palm trees and wild bird of paradise flowers (I picked many), we arrived at a beautiful cove with a white sand beach and crystal clear water. After collecting seashells and going skinny-dipping, we decided to head back.

I looked up at the sky and told Steve we had better hurry as the clouds looked threatening. He said the storm was hours away, but I was not convinced. We were half way back, in the thick of the jungle, when the wind started and it got black as night. Trees started falling all around and torrential rain came at us sideways. I was sure I was going to die. But nothing would prepare me for what we saw when we arrived back to the beach where we had left our dinghy. The calm cove we had been anchored in had turned into a raging sea with six to eight foot breakers hitting the beach. *Poet's Place*, along with *Vite*, was riding the waves like a bucking bronco, both bows buried under the sea. Steve had to scream over the wind, rain and sea to tell me he didn't think we could both make it back to the boat. He said he might be able to row the dinghy through the high seas alone and I would stay on the beach until the storm was over. It was awful watching him row through the waves and then get aboard the boat. I found a little thatched tree house that Filo's family built and decided to wait out the storm there. I was shivering from the cold and drenched from the rain when Filo's dog found me and started barking; which brought Filo to the tree house to investigate. He insisted I come with him to his modest thatched roof, dirt floor home on the other side of the beach. Once in the warmth of his home, his wife gave me a dry T-shirt and fed me a lobster and rice dinner. They then gave me pineapple, avocados, limes and bananas (all grown on the island) to take back to the boat. I had a wonderful time with this generous family and by the time Steve returned after the storm, he no longer felt sorry for leaving me on the beach. We spent a couple of weeks anchored off this island and getting to know Filo and his family of lobster fishermen.

We moved on to Gamez Island where again we were in paradise, with white sandy beach, clear turquoise water and swaying palms. It's a narrow little island so you can see from one side to the other. There was a beautiful breeze blowing through the island, so we hung our hammocks between the palm trees and enjoyed taking naps in the shade of the swaying palms while watching the yellow canaries fly by. And this is how our German friends on *S/V Germania* found us as they pulled into the anchorage. It was a great reunion, as we had not seen them for several months. We enjoyed more snorkeling, diving, spear fishing and seafood dinners. We stayed there for a few more weeks.

We left *Germania* at Gamez and sailed to the Secas Islands. When we arrived, *Vite* was leaving, but showed us where they swam with the turtles. The next day we snorkeled the area and I too got to swim with the giant sea turtles. It was awesome to stare face to face with the big giants. They didn't seem to be scared at all. We did some of our best diving and spear fishing here. While at the Secas I rescued a brand new baby coconut palm tree. They grow right out of the coconut. It just splits open and out come these little palm leaves. This one had only four leaves. I just picked her up off the beach, named her Palma, put her in a small container with some dirt and sand and placed her in the cockpit (much to Steve's protest). In four months, Palma grew three feet, had fourteen leaves and lived in a new bucket in our cockpit. I figure, about the time our shade awning was worn out, Palma would be big enough to provide us shade. Steve continued to protest, but I loved having a tree in my cockpit. This is also the place where our computer crashed and so did I.

We visited several more beautiful, secluded islands before arriving at Bahia Honda, a lush, tranquil, remote bay on the mainland of Panama. Here, the native Indians live on a little island in the bay just as they did one-hundred years ago. There are no roads in or out of this place. The only way here is by boat and the only mode of transportation is dugout canoe. Everyone has one. Some families have two or three. The kids paddle them all over. As we dropped anchor, we were surrounded by dugouts bringing gifts of bananas, peppers, oranges and other local fruit to trade for sugar, powdered milk and any other items they seldom see. These people truly live off the land. Most of the natives have never left the area and have never seen a town or store. We felt as though we had gone back in time. But things may change for Bahia Honda, as an American from New York has purchased some property and is building a couple of homes. The locals are being hired for construction jobs and are making money for the first time. This will change everything. I'm not so sure it will be for the better. The people have lived off the land for centuries and have everything they need for their simple lifestyle. They fish, gather fruit, build their homes and dugouts and are happy. Now they have money and will want to have more stuff and their life will no longer be simple. Someday they may have a life full of things and have to work to pay for them. They will have stress and live the life we left behind so we could experience their laid-back lifestyle. We feel privileged to have visited Bahia Honda while it is still untouched by civilization.

We made friends with a local man named Domingo, who would row out to our boat everyday and talk with us (in Spanish only) about the changes the younger locals liked and he did not. During one of our conversations, we found out that he and I share the exact same birthday; month, day and year. Of course I look much younger (maybe it was his missing teeth), but it was a very strange feeling.

At Bahia Honda we met John who lives on his sailboat and heads the construction project there. By this time *Germania* had caught up with us. We hadn't seen a store of any kind for over two months. Great for the budget, but I get tired of baking my own bread. John's company has a high-speed motorboat that makes trips into the town of Santiago a couple times a week. It's about a three hour ride up a river and then a two-hour bus ride into the city. He offered the four of us a ride so we could shop and visit the town. We all jumped at the chance. The boat ride was a hoot and the town of Santiago was a shock with big buildings, malls, McDonalds and K.F.C. We thought we were back in the States. We stayed three days and two nights at a nice hotel and really enjoyed stocking up on items we hadn't seen in months. We also had a computer store look at our computer and tell us what we already suspected—it was too old to fix. Better the computer than me, but a big disappointment.

Our stay in Bahia Honda was over three weeks and before we left, Domingo rowed out to our boat with a gift of three handmade wooden bowls; a gift I will treasure and keep forever. It was difficult to leave this beautiful bay and all the new friends we made, but we needed to move on. We explored several more beautiful, remote islands sharing with friends on *Germania*, walking beaches, collecting shells and flowers, trading with the shrimp boats for buckets of shrimp and diving for dinner. We slowly made our way towards Cape Mala which is known for its high wind and seas. Both boats sailed the two-day passage around Cape Mala through twenty-five knot winds, rough seas and the shipping lanes to the Panama Canal. We counted twenty-six ships one night.

 It was great to finally arrive at Isla San Jose, one of the beautiful islands of the Las Perlas in the Bay of Panama. On this almost remote island lives *Mr. Robinson Caruso* whose name is Dieter. He and his wife Gerta sailed from Germany twenty years ago, stayed on this island and have never left. They have a small farm with fruit trees, chickens, sheep, pigs and two dogs. They welcome cruisers and loved *Germania* as they could all speak German. They were fun characters. We really enjoyed our visit. How they can live in such a remote fashion, without any friends or neighbors, is beyond me. Steve thought it was great. I think it's crazy and I would go berserk with only animals and a husband to talk with.

Steve
Dieter was a strange German Nazi character still hiding out from World War II and gleefully told stories about shooting at American planes during the war. He was still into guns, as he often carried a shotgun and set many booby trap devices with exploding shotgun

shells to kill wild pigs on his property. We had to really watch where we stepped. He actually did not own any property. He just sort of squatted there; building a Robinson Caruso type house and claiming that part of the island for himself. The locals stayed clear of him for fear of him and his pig traps. Dieter was seventy-one years old but as I followed him on a hike around the island one day it seemed like he was twenty. I could hardly keep up with him as he ran bare foot through the jungle. Deiter and his wife were very intelligent people and we had many interesting conversations. They were starved for outside contact and begged us to stay. After three days of intense visiting we were ready to move on and sailed away; looking back at the beautiful sand beach on their remote little island.

Sharon

The anchorage at Isla Pedro Gonzales was one of the most beautiful anchorages I have ever seen. It had a glistening long white sand beach with lush jungle in the background and sparkling clear water. We shared this anchorage with five other boats. This was the most boats we'd seen in one anchorage since Costa Rica. There were three French boats, one Spanish boat, one German boat, and us from the U.S. The French ladies went topless, so Steve's binoculars got a workout! The guys all built a smoker on the beach and smoked their catch using coconut husk. It was so delicious. We gathered limes and mangos to share. The common language was English or Spanish and all the other cruisers spoke three or four languages. Americans are so bad when it comes to learning languages.

A few more islands, a few more anchorage's and then we arrived at Isla Contadora, or was I in Southern California? This lovely island is populated with wealthy homes and a few hotels. Several of the buildings are owned by Panamanians, some by American and some European. It was sort of nice to be in civilization again. Contadora is a nice mix of local and American type homes and restaurants. It has a couple of small stores, a small airport and lots of nice roads for walking. It has the feel of a small town and we really liked the people. Everyone was friendly and very helpful. We met a German guy named Gunter on Contadora who is a big ham radio operator. We visited his gorgeous home up on a hill overlooking the ocean and his ham radio room that looked like the NASA Space Center control room. He is a great help to cruisers crossing the Pacific as his signal reaches across the ocean. At his home, we met Herb, another ham guy from the Galapagos who was visiting and he extended us an invitation to visit him when we get to the Galapagos. It's sure a wonderful world full of interesting people.

9-11-2001

It was during our stay on Contadora that the World Trade Center was hit and we were able to see some of it on television at the hotel. It was very sad indeed. We had no lack of news on this event. We listened to the BBC, German news and Russian news (all in English). It was interesting to get other countries perspective on the event. I sometimes think we are safer out here than back in the States and we are glad to be cruising and experiencing other cultures.

Steve

Most Americans were shocked that someone would want to do such a dastardly deed to the U.S., the land of democracy and freedom. But we have seen firsthand many heinous deeds done by the U.S. to the people of Central America, from propping up greedy dictators to invading and bombing Panama. Many innocent people here lost their lives as a direct or indirect result of U.S. Foreign Policy. I know our State Department would have us believe our Foreign Policy is to promote freedom and democracy, but we have found that not to be the case. In talking to many people from other countries we find they are sympathetic, but not surprised that we were attacked in this manner. We seem to be our own worst enemy as we lay off thousands of U.S. workers. While merchants here in Panama were begging for U.S. products, they could not get them through our new tight security systems.

Sharon

After three months of cruising the remote islands of Panama, we sailed to Panama City and dropped anchor off Flamenco Island. This little island is connected to Balboa (beautiful suburb of the city) by a lovely causeway. It reminds me of San Diego. There is a two mile paved walk along the water that is lighted at night for walking, biking or roller-skating. There are a couple of nice restaurants and great bus connections to the city. We have a beautiful unobstructed view of the skyline of Panama City on one side, and the ship traffic as it enters the canal on the other. At night the lights of the city are magical. There were about twelve other boats here and we often share taxi and bus rides as well as potluck dinners. It is a great place to be since almost anything you need is in Panama. The U.S. used to occupy the canal area bringing many American products to Panama. It's sad to see all the empty houses left by the U.S. Being here gives us the opportunity to get needed boat parts, do provisioning and take care of medical and dental needs.

Poet's Place **(crew only) goes through the Canal**

It is an interesting mix of boats at the anchorage; some came through the canal from Europe or the Caribbean, some were waiting to go through from the Pacific and still others waited for favorable weather to head to Ecuador or to the South Pacific. The atmosphere is exciting and the anchorage is like a little neighborhood with everyone helping everyone. Every boat that goes through the canal needs six people, four line handlers, the skipper and someone in the galley to feed the crew. Most boats consist of couples, so if they are going through the canal they need four more people. You can hire line handlers, but that gets expensive and all the cruisers want the experience of going through the canal before they take their own boat through. Even if we aren't going through with our own boat, we all want the experience.

Steve and I were quick to volunteer as line handlers for our friends. We have many friends and Steve makes a great line handler, so we have been in great demand. So far, we have transited the canal on three different boats. It is a very long, exciting and stressful day.

91

The boats usually leave our anchorage about 5:00 a.m., pick up the pilot (provided by the canal) and then start the trip through Balboa, under the *Bridge of the Americas* and into the Miraflores locks, of which there are two. In the locks, a sailboat is usually, but not always, tied alongside a tug. There is sometimes a huge container ship in front of you. Things get a little tense when the locks fill and there is lots of turbulence. The line handlers are making sure the lines holding the sailboat to the tug are secure and need to know when to tie up and un-tie. When the container ship moves out of the lock, her prop makes more turbulence and it is sometimes difficult to handle the boat. Things can get a little tense, but a good crew really helps. One then enters Miraflores Lake where the Pedro Miguel Boat Club is located. We joined the club for fifteen dollars and therefore attend the potlucks and use the facilities. A bus ride takes us there from our anchorage. Some boats stay here for several weeks or months until a later date when they continue the canal transit. This club no longer exists since Panama took over the canal.

Boats going to the other side continue through the third set of locks, the Pedro Miguel locks and enter the Culebra Cut. This body of water is a narrow stretch in the canal extending from the Pedro Miguel Locks to Gamboa and crosses the Continental Divide. It is 12.6 kilometers long. One then enters Gatun Lake, which is scattered with little islands and is very scenic.

One can even view monkeys hanging from the trees on the islands. It takes about five to six hours, depending on the boat, to motor across the lake. This is when the crew usually eats, as it is a more relaxing time than locking through. Once through the lake, the boat enters the Gatum Locks, of which there are three. The first three locks, you lock up, the locks then fill and you go up. With the three Gatum locks you lock down, the locks empty and you go down. Once through the Gatum locks you enter the Atlantic. It is very exciting at this point, having gone from the Pacific side to the Atlantic and everyone is usually cheering. The boat then pulls into Colon to disembark the tired crew who take a bus or cab back to Panama City and the anchorage.

Most boats can make the transit in one long day, usually arriving in Colon around 6:00 p.m. The slower boats take two days, spending a night anchored in Gatun Lake. The Canal is approximately sixty miles long. The transit, for a sailboat our size at that time costs $500 plus an $800 deposit, which you got back once you had completed the transit.

Poet's Place was still on the Pacific side of Panama waiting for many things. Our daughter, Michelle and her boyfriend, Leon will be visiting the end of November, bringing with them many items we need for the boat plus a family fix for me. We are more than a little homesick. We hope to take them sailing to the Las Perlas islands, but who knows, maybe they will transit the canal with us. Part of cruising is changing plans and ours are changing almost daily. Health and family are most important to us and due to the stock market crash, we may need to work out here somewhere.

My Tapestry

Sharon Reed-Hendricks

My life is like a tapestry
The colors woven in
Of paths that cross and lives that touch
And places I have been

Of lessons learned and faces
Of those that touch my heart
We sometimes take a different path
Sometimes we drift apart

The people in my life have been
The tapestry I weave
They're woven in part of my life
Even after they leave

The colors of my tapestry
All mix together so
I see why people touch my life
And why some had to go

And I have learned in letting go
I'm free to spread my wings
The beauty of my tapestry
Has shown me many things

8 Passage to Ecuador and The Pirate Encounter

Panama City is truly a crossroads and there are many choices of direction for a boat to take. We changed our minds daily as to which way we should go—left into the Caribbean or right to the Pacific. We just couldn't decide, so we went straight ahead and here we are in Ecuador, South America. But I think I should back up a little first and go back to Panama to catch you up.

Our daughter, Michelle and her boyfriend, Leon were scheduled to arrive the end of November for a two-week visit when our refrigerator quit (yes, our series of events was continuing). They were able to change their flight to the beginning of December, so they could bring the refrigerator compressor with them along with two huge duffel bags of boat parts. It was great to see Michelle and Leon and the needed boat parts. Steve spent the first few days of their visit installing new parts. The three weeks before Michelle arrived, Steve and I were busy earning money to help pay for the needed boat parts. Steve helped three boats during haul-out and I did some canvas sewing. We earned enough to pay for the boat parts and replenish the kitty. Along with our many boat parts, was a new digital camera, a Christmas gift from Michelle and Tracy, so we can take pictures once again.

We sailed back to the Las Perlas Islands to enjoy them with the kids. We had a great time spear fishing and smoking our catch in the smoker we constructed at Don Bernardo anchorage a few months earlier with the French boats. We ate smoked fish, drank fresh coconut milk from the trees, snorkeled, beach combed and just enjoyed the islands.

Steve
Here are some instructions on making a Panamanian Fish Smoker; first find an old rusty fifty gallon barrel washed up on the beach,

95

cut the top off to use for a lid. Punch or drill some small holes around the upper edge to string some stainless steel wire across to make hanging racks. Punch some bigger holes in the top to let the smoke flow through and cut a twelve inch square fire door in the side, near the ground. Gather some old coconut husk for burning in the bottom of the barrel, they will just slowly smolder all day and give a nice flavor and golden color to the fish. We cut the fish in thin strips and soak it in spicy salt brine for at least twelve hours before smoking. About five hours in the smoker does it. If you do it right and keep it in a dry place it will keep for weeks.

Sharon

We had a great visit with Michelle and Leon, both in the islands and in Panama City shopping. There are great buys in Panama, especially from the Kuna Indians and they were able to get their Christmas shopping done while there.

The Kuna women dress very colorfully. Apart from golden rings in their noses, breast plates, intricate bead work on their arms and legs, face painting and orange scarves, the most eye catching item is their blouse or mola with intricately designed and sewn panels. These reverse appliqué designs are quite famous and sell worldwide. It takes a Kuna woman sometimes a week to make one mola. We were able to buy a mola for just a few dollars but understand they can sell for eighty dollars or more in some places. Needless to say, I bought several for gifts to take home when we visit.

As always, there were lots of tears when we had to say goodbye to Michelle and Leon. They are both looking forward to their next visit in the South Seas. We already have a new list of needed boat parts started for their next visit.

Steve and I had wanted to do some inland travel in Panama since we arrived, but due to medical needs and the many boat parts to fix we just didn't find the time. After Michelle left and Christmas was approaching, we thought this might be a good time to go as we were feeling homesick. We had heard so many wonderful things about the mountain town of Boquete from other cruisers that we headed for the mountains. And beautiful it is. Boquete Valley is located in the fertile Western highlands of Panama. Here in the cloud forest, the moisture and the volcanic soil combine with ideal growing conditions to produce some of the world's best coffee. It was cool up in these mountains and we needed jackets everyday and two blankets on the bed at night. We found a charming little chalet where we had the room on the second floor with a balcony looking out over the river and the flower gardens. It was breath-taking, and only sixteen dollars a night (I like these prices). We had our own bathroom with plenty of hot water and big fluffy towels. We visited the coffee plantation and bought coffee for gifts and rented bikes one day to enjoy the enchanting village. It was just what we needed to get-away and relax after all the boat work. I know it may sound funny to our readers that we need to get away when it must seem like we are away on this adventure. I use to think that too, before I began cruising, but cruising is a lifestyle not a vacation. We are always working on something, whether it's a repair on the boat, washing laundry in a bucket or taking all day to din-ghy and walk miles to the market to buy food. The simplest things can take all day, so we need to get away from the boat just as land-lubbers need to get away from their house. But unlike landlub-bers, we need to first find a safe and affordable place to leave the boat before we can go anywhere. So in-land travel is our need-ed little vacation away from the boat.

Christmas is always difficult being away from family, so cruisers always get together to create our own extended family celebration. This Christmas was no different as about twelve other cruising boats got together for a Christmas Eve potluck and white elephant gift exchange. We always have wonderful food and great laughs with the gift exchange. One couple even wrapped up their pet cat, complete with litter box. Glad we didn't get that one.

Flamenco Island, with its panoramic view of Panama City, was the best place to be anchored for the New Year's Eve fireworks. What a show! Fireworks in every direction and they lasted for at least an hour. We had the best seats and we didn't even have to go anywhere. It was now year 2002.

Panama City was beginning to feel like home, we had been there so long. The boats in the anchorage were calling me the *Chamber of Commerce* since I knew where to get everything in the city. I even arranged shopping trips to the market and arranged for one of the largest Costco-type stores to bring a van to take us shopping to their store. On one such trip we had over twenty cruisers and two kids and so they sent a school bus that time. I also joined an English speaking 12-step AA group and was privileged to meet many local and U.S. Embassy people who are now good friends. I was beginning to feel like this was my new home. Not only was it difficult to say "till we meet again" to so many cruising friends who went through the canal into the Caribbean, but also to so many new friends in Panama City. Lots of tears were shed when we finally pulled our anchor to head to Ecuador. We had been in Panama City and the Perlas Islands for over four months. The weather window was here and it was time to go. We were headed for French Polynesia by way of Ecuador and the Galapagos.

Before leaving on the passage to Ecuador, Nancy from S/V *Nanjo* and I went fruit and veggie shopping and split a sack of 100 oranges, a stalk of 250 green bananas and many other items. We had enough produce to feed a navy carrier. Anyway, we hung our stalk of 125 bananas under the solar-panel arch, over Palma my fast-growing coconut palm tree. It all looked very tropical.

We sailed first to the Perlas Islands to do some fishing and snorkeling and say goodbye to the Islands I love so much. On Sunday January 27th we left San Jose Island with a strong thirty knot northerly wind and very confused seas. The first twenty-four hours were not fun; at least not for me and for cooking in the galley. If you ask Steve, he will tell you it was a wonderful sail. The sailboat *Nanjo* had left Panama City a few hours before and we would be in radio contact and sometimes visual contact, the entire passage. Both boats made over one-hundred-sixty miles the first day. We also checked into the *Pacific Seafarer's Ham Radio Net* every night to give them our position and weather conditions. This was a big comfort to me to hear the voices of these guys every night and to know someone out there knew where we were. They tracked our position daily on their web site so family and friends back home could follow our trip. We will do this again when we cross to the Galapagos and also from the Galapagos to the South Pacific. The six-day six-night passage wasn't bad. We had some rain, some calms, some wind and some sunshine, a little of everything—including little sleep. This is the most difficult part of any passage for me is the lack of sleep. It's like having a baby. Every three hours or so you get up and take a watch. About the time you're falling asleep and you're not sure if the lights on the horizon are stars or a freighter, you wake the other person and you crash for three hours, then repeat the process all over again. In between all this you prepare and eat a few meals, plot your position, do your radio contacts, make a few sail changes and try to remember why it is you are out here. And people wonder what we do on these long passages.

For entertainment on this passage we had our bananas. When green bananas turn yellow, they all seem to turn at once. What to do with one-hundred ripe bananas? Well, we had banana pancakes, banana oatmeal, banana bread, banana pudding, fried bananas and bananas and oranges (don't forget the fifty oranges). Bananas and fish are good too. I'm thinking of writing a banana cookbook on 101 ways to use bananas. And poor Palma (the palm tree) had an identity crisis. As the bananas started turning black and falling into Palma's pot, she thought she was a banana tree instead of a coconut palm. Steve was having a fit because everything on the back deck was slippery from the bananas. We never went hungry for fruit.

Pirates Approach Off of Colombia

On Thursday January 31th about mid-morning, I was in the cockpit on watch and Steve was on the radio with *Nanjo* when out of no where, two-hundred miles off the shore of Colombia, a high speed panga (twenty-four foot open boat) appeared on our port side with five men aboard. I forgot for a moment that I was off shore and waved hello like I do to the fishermen around the islands. These were not fishermen. They first asked for cigarettes and beer and I said no, we did not smoke. They then asked for fuel and again I said no. They asked for water and then seeing our bananas, they asked for them and I threw a few black ones to them. This was all spoken in Spanish. Steve stayed below on the radio and said that *Nanjo* was turning around (they were a few miles ahead of us) and heading our way. The panga continued to get closer to our port side and they became very aggressive. The man in the front of the panga reached out and grabbed our lifeline and started to lift his leg to board our boat. At this point I got scared as a few months ago, off the coast of Venezuela, another cruising boat was approached the same way and asked for water and cigarettes. When they were told no, the pirate came aboard and the pirate shot the husband on the cruising boat. The husband survived but it was a terrible event in the cruising community. Just as one of the men were about to board our boat, their panga stopped dead in the water and our boat continued to sail away.

I thought at first they were out of fuel, but Steve had another idea and when he pulled in our fishing line that we always troll when underway, he saw it was severed. The line is three-hundred pound test nylon cord and it fouled the propeller causing their outboard to stall. We lost a good lure and some line, but we have our lives. We now have a new weapon on board—our fishing line. I don't know if they would have hurt us if they came aboard, as I saw no weapons. However I have no doubt they would have boarded us and asked for anything and everything and there were five of them and only two of us. I am so glad we were dragging that fishing line and that *Nanjo* was so close to us. We never saw that boat or pirates again but we did report it on the *ham net* that evening.

Crossing the Equator

On Friday February 1st, 2002 at 6:30p.m. silhouetted by a beautiful sunset, we crossed the equator and entered the Southern Hemisphere. What a thrill! *Nanjo* had slowed down so that we could take pictures of each other's boats as we crossed. All afternoon we had a blue-footed booby bird perched on our bow rail. We think Neptune sent him to guide us across the equator. We had flat seas and a gentle breeze and whales swimming beside the boats, and of course, the blue-footed booby. It was magical! King Neptune was good to us so we celebrated with a bottle of sparkling cider someone had given us over two years ago when we left Seattle. We shared the contents with Neptune and the booby. We also popped some popcorn and enjoyed the evening watching a beautiful sunset. But Neptune tricked us because the next day we had rain and nasty weather. Everything is not upside-down in the Southern Hemisphere as one may think. We do not have to stand on our heads to see the sky. You do however, have to watch your navigation as latitudes run from north to south instead of south to north.

After a six-day six-night passage, we arrived in Bahia de Caraquez Ecuador on Saturday February 2nd. We had to wait outside the river bar for the Port Captain's office to send a pilot out to lead us in, where three other cruising boats were already anchored up the picturesque river. Bahia (as the locals call it) is a quintessential sleepy little town with very friendly locals. In fact a week or so after we arrived, we had eight boats anchored in the river and the Mayor of the town had a welcoming party for all the cruisers and presented us with certificates along with a guided tour of the area in an open truck bus. We were all treated like royalty. In the past, very few cruising boats stopped in Bahia. In fact until this season, they hadn't seen a boat in over eight months. Bahia also has a number of inexpensive restaurants and stores.

Everything in Ecuador is cheap. The food is cheap and very good, so we ate out all the time. The down side is that you have to be careful because you cannot drink the water anywhere in Ecuador unless it's bottled or boiled. Parasites and amoebas are a fact of life here. Also, it's the rainy season in Ecuador (January-April) and it just started. It just ended in Panama and Costa Rica and lasted nine months, so we've been following the rain and I'm sick of it! This is why I left Seattle.

Our reason for coming to Ecuador was to travel inland, especially into the Andes. Bahia turned out to be a very safe place to leave the boat to do this. The boats were anchored in front of the Port Captain's office and we took turns traveling in-land so there was always someone to look after the boats. We had three boats from the U.S. three from England, one from Canada, and one from Australia. At the time of this writing, seven of the boats have traveled in-land and three were robbed at the bus station or on buses out of Quito, and three people got sick from the food. So in-land travel in Ecuador is a little riskier than most places. We understand Peru is worse. Steve and I felt very fortunate, as we never got sick or robbed. We kept our backpacks with us at all times while traveling and kept money and passports in a money belt. Our friends on *Nanjo* who traveled with us were not so fortunate, as they were robbed on the bus from Quito to Guaranda. They had placed their bag in the overhead on the bus and the thieves got John's (he is an insulin dependent diabetic) test kit for his blood sugar, along with several other items. Luckily, they did not take his insulin, but he was guessing as to how much insulin to take. This incident cut our trip to only a week, when we were planning on two. However, we were ready to return to the boat at this point as we were all tired and a little bummed.

Now for the good part. Ecuador inland is breathtakingly beautiful, friendly (except for the robbers) and rich with history and crafts. Quito, the capital city, dates back to pre-Colombian times. Set in the mountains, it is quite cool despite the fact it is on the equator. We enjoyed a couple of days touring around the old town and viewing the stunning colonial buildings. We then traveled north across the equator (again) to the small town of Otavalo, which is famous for its market that dates back to pre-Inca times. The Otavaleno people are very distinctive as the men have long ponytails, reversible ponchos and dark felt hats. The women also are very striking in their beautiful embroidered blouses, shawls and head cloths and gold necklaces. They are famous for their weavings, which are for sale everywhere on market day. They are woven on a hand worked loom and are extremely beautiful and very inexpensive here but quite expensive in the States. I bought several woven tapestries for gifts. The whole place reminded me of Antigue Guatemala and I fell in love with it. The other item they are famous for are their Alpaca jackets made of Llama wool. They are very beautiful and not so cheap, however much cheaper than anywhere else. I was able to negotiate a good price as I bought five little Alpaca jackets, one for each grandchild. We have got to make a trip home soon as we have so many gifts and not much room on the boat. After Otavalo, we once again crossed the equator and traveled south where the massive range of the Andes neatly divides the country. To the east lie the jungles of the upper Amazon Basin, and to the west are the coastal lowlands. The western drop of the Andes is dramatic. The scenery is breathtaking, we even saw herds of wild llamas, but I was freezing. The charming little town, high in the mountains where we stayed was just too cold for me. The best hotel in town had no hot water and no heat so my memories of this area are a little frosty. Steve however loved the cool mountain air and enjoyed this area more than I. Inland travel in Ecuador is very inexpensive. The hotels we stayed at cost between eight and twelve dollars per night for two people. Meals on the average ran about $1.50 per person for a full meal. Ecuador also uses the American dollar for their currency.

Steve

We rode buses over 1,000 miles from sea level up to 12,000 feet. The roads we traveled had few cars but lots of other hazards like trucks, herds of cows, sheep, llamas, pigs and donkeys. There were also many mudslides that damaged the roads and it was common to have big rocks in the road that had fallen from cliffs high above or areas where the road had completely washed away and we had to make our own road. The bus drivers all drove like hell, trying to pass anyone who got in front of them. We tried not to look, as the driver would pass trucks going uphill on blind curves and then meet another bus coming down the hill. The two outside vehicles would then drive off the shoulder just in time, as we passed in between with horns honking and lights flashing. The buses were sometimes crowded and when they could not pack another body inside they put people on the roof, where it's cooler and you get a better view. They have one driver and one or two swampers/conductors, who pack the people in, load baggage, take the money and negotiate traffic tickets for the driver. This has to be one of the great bus rides of the world but not for "the faint of heart".

Sharon

We have really enjoyed Ecuador and have gone broke saving money on all the inexpensive items. We are setting sail in a few days for the Galapagos Islands and I can hardly wait. It has been a lifetime dream of mine to visit these islands and their unique wildlife. We plan to stay about a month visiting the different islands before heading across the Pacific on our longest ocean passage. We will be crossing from the Galapagos to French Polynesia.

S/V Poet's Place   **Shopping in Mazatlan**

Daughter Michelle and Sharon at Las Tres Marietas

105

Sharon and Steve in Antigua Guatemala

Guatemala

**Making tortillas in
El Salvador**

Fish speared in Sea of Cortez

Fishermen of Fanning Island

Steve smoking fish on a beach in Panama

Our three part nested dinghy

Baby sea lions play in our dinghy in the Galapagos

Rowing everywhere was our best exercise

Water falls on
Fatu Hiva

Dolphins off
our bow

Swimming under-
way to keep cool

Landfall at Fatu Hiva, French Polynesia (aka Bay of Penises)

Poets Place, **Anchored at Hiva Oa, French Polynesia**

Motorcycle touring in Rarotonga

Dinghy landing on the island nation of Niue

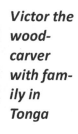

Victor the wood-carver with family in Tonga

Poet's Place with a fresh paint job - Bay of Islands New Zealand

Sheep shearing on our friend Ian's farm

Local New Zealand doctor makes house calls at the boat yard, checking sun damaged skin.

Steve finds an old cannon on a remote island in Fiji

Tapa cloth gift from a family in Fiji

Dancers on Robinson Crusoe Island, Fiji

Bike hike on Fanning Island

Tranquility of Fanning Island

The idyllic South Seas Island, Fanning Atoll is just 1,000 miles south of Hawaii

My Love Has Wings

Sharon Reed-Hendricks

I must say good-bye for now
You may not understand
This path, which I must follow
Is alone without your hand

But I will leave you with a gift
To share and give away
The poetry I leave with you
Are the words I cannot say

The words I cannot always find
Until I write them down
My poetry will always be
These feelings I have found

To tell you that I really care
And that I love you so
Yet when our paths go separate ways
Sometimes we have to go

We all are given gifts in life
And the greatest gift to give
Is love- with a set of wings
And to just let go - and live

9 The Galapagos Islands and The 28 Day Ocean Passage

Sharon

It was difficult to say goodbye to Ecuador, especially Bahia De Caraquez where we were anchored up the river in front of the charming town. The prices were cheap, the people friendly, the food was great and the weather was good, however Steve says it was too hot. Upon finding out that I was a poet, the Port Captain asked for a copy of my book, which I proudly autographed for him. He loves poetry and was trying to learn English, so the book was greatly appreciated. As we left Bahia De Caraquez to head for Ecuador, and were about two miles out of the river, there came a call on our VHF radio. "*Poet's Place, Poet's Place*, this is the Port Captain." All I could think of was that we had done something wrong. Then he started to recite one of my poems in English. It was the poem about good-byes, and it brought tears to my eyes. He ended with: "Have a good sail and please return to Bahia De Caraquez someday." By this time I was crying so much I could hardly talk. Goodbyes are never easy.

We had a comfortable eight-day sail to Wreck Bay on San Cristobal Island in the Galapagos. We anchored with six other boats, all from other countries, which became the norm from here on. Many times throughout the Pacific, we were the only American boat and so we got to thoroughly enjoy the company of the Europeans and the British.

San Cristobal Island was a beautiful place with a charming little town and more sea lions than people. It was like animal soup, there were so many sea lions. They think they own the place (which they do). You cannot leave your dinghy in the water at night because by morning there would be sea lions making it their new home. They sunk our dinghy one night as they had a difficult time jumping into the nested hard dory. They even jumped onto some of the boats and into their cockpits. They get very upset when one tries to get them off. It was a riot to watch them. They entertained the entire fleet. It was easy to swim with them, as they are thick in the clear water. The other interesting animal at San Cristobal was the marina iguana. They're so ugly they're cute, in a prehistoric way. They let you get as close as you want (like they're posing) to take pictures. We got some great photos. Although sometimes they spit at you and it happened to Steve.

We visited with Herb, a friend we met in Panama, who lives in San Cristobal. He took us on a tour with two other cruising boats (English and Australian) up to the volcano and around the island. It was beautiful. We also shared lunch with him every day at the local restaurant. The lunch special was $1.50 for soup, main meal and drink.

Everyday we walked into town and I stopped to talk with Peppi, the 150-year-old giant tortoise who lived behind the Catholic Church. He would slowly crawl to the fence to be petted and talked with. He loved attention and begged to be fed. His favorite food was bread from the bakery and he seemed to know where I was going each morning. I would feed him a bit of bread and then say, "I've got to go Peppi, goodbye." He would turn around and slowly walk away. I would feel so badly that I would say, "Okay Peppi, you can have some more." And honestly, that tortoise would turn around and run back to the fence for more bread. I never knew a tortoise could be so endearing.

We stayed three weeks on San Cristobal and during that time I received an email that my mom had died. She had not been well for about six months and was 89 years old, so it was a blessing, but still difficult to bear, especially being so far away. I don't think we are ever prepared for the death of a parent. I was unable to fly home as flights out of San Cristobal are only twice a week and one must go to Ecuador to connect with the U.S. Time and costs were not on my side, so I did my grieving with nature and the animals of the Galapagos (very fitting for me). I would swim and talk with the animals and cry. I felt guilt and anger, sorrow and pain. I was sad that I wasn't there but happy that I had spent some time with her when we visited from Mexico. She was always excited to hear our ham radio contacts when we could talk about our adventures. She loved to travel and was living the adventures through me. She would always ask questions about the places we were and about the animals and the people. She was proud of me that I was on this journey and told me how she wished she could have taken a journey like ours. So I took her with me in my heart and I shared my journey with her in spirit.

After three weeks at Wreck Bay, we sailed to Isla Isabela and anchored at Villamil. For me, Isabela was the best of the Galapagos. The little village of Villamil is charming. There are no tourists and more animals than all the other islands put together. It was magical. We saw and touched penguins on the rocks near our anchorage, swam and played with the baby sea lions, touched and fed the giant tortoise, played with sea turtles, watched pink flamingos fly by the boat and walked with the marina iguanas in the sand.

There were about twelve other boats from all over the world and many talented cruisers. We spent many nights at the large pink house on the beach playing music, the international language. The pink house was a hotel converted into a lovely Spanish style home with large iguanas hanging from the rafters and belonged to an interesting young couple. The young man was an attorney from Texas and his wife was from Argentina. They had a set of triplet boys and a baby daughter. They loved the cruisers and invited us to their home several times a week for dinner and music. The attorney from Texas played the guitar along with the cruiser from Denmark. The Frenchman played the harmonica, the Portuguese played drums and the couple from Spain strummed the Spanish guitar while she sang. There was magic in the air. On one of those nights, the Port Captain joined us (he is a poet); he and I recited poetry.

119

While on Isabela I lost a filling in a tooth, so we put out a call for a dentist. The captain on a French boat was a dentist but he did not have his tools. I had some tools, thanks to a visit from our dentist friend Barry and a cruiser from Brazil had the filling material. We asked permission to use the town clinic and off we went. By this time, there were three other cruisers that needed dental work and so an afternoon was spent at the dental clinic. Payment was as followed: Steve fixed the French boat's refrigerator, someone else gave the dentist a CD of his music and one of the ladies baked him a cake. I love the barter system. The world should take lessons from the cruising community.

One day we went horse-back riding into the active volcano on Isabela with eight other cruisers. We had a wonderful time, sharing lunch on top of the volcano.

Steve
For fifteen dollars we rented horses and a guide to explore the large volcano that makes up most of Isabela. The horses were sturdy and well trained; they hardly broke a sweat on the trail up the mountain. The horse bridals were made of just rope and the saddles were made of old tires, inner tubes and rope. The riding equipment looked crude but all worked well. The scenery was spectacular as we rode where few people ever travel. We road to the top of Sierra Negra, Galápagos a volcano with a crater more than five miles across, steaming with hot lava.

Sharon
I really didn't want to leave the Galapagos, but I wanted to see the South Pacific and it was time to go. I was also in trouble with the Port Captain and needed to exit. You see, I'm a natural net-worker (talker) and while talking on the radio net one night, another cruiser heading this way asked me, which places in the Galapagos were the best to visit. Without hesitation I said, "Skip the rest and just come to Isabela. The island has everything; iguanas, giant tortoise, sea turtles, flamingos, penguins and sea lions, also friendly people,

cheap meals and no tourists. The Port Captain is wonderful and lets you stay as long as you wish, unlike the other Galapagos Islands where you can only stay a few weeks. This place is what you dream about when you think of the Galapagos." Well, being the good salesperson that I am, everyone listening on the radio net that night that was heading to the Galapagos pulled anchor and sailed directly for Isabela. Within a week we had thirty boats anchored in the harbor at Isabela and the Port Captain was in trouble with the Ecuadorian government (they own the Galapagos Islands) for allowing boats to stay indefinitely and not collecting a fee. He wanted to know who let everyone know about Isabela? It was time to leave.

Every day, two to four boats left for the long ocean crossing, there were over thirty of us; so we started the *Coconut Breakfast Net* and kept track of each other's progress. In the morning at about 8:00 a.m. we checked into the net, this got quite difficult as the time zones changed about four times as we crossed. Everyone was on a different time depending on where you were. Thank goodness for ZULU time (GMT, Greenwich Mean Time) because after a while you didn't know what day it was, but it was a comfort to know there were others out there on the big ocean.

Steve and I are on the same boat but we experience very different trips. Steve loves to sail and sail hard. I tolerate it. Steve loves passages and I like landfalls. Steve enjoys quiet and I enjoy talking and need people to talk with—the more, the better. It took twenty-eight long, lonely days to reach the Marquises in French Polynesia. Here is what it's like to be out to sea on a small sailboat for twenty-eight days.

Sharon's Trip
It's not much fun and I hate passages. I like to go for walks, swim, bike ride and visit with people. None of these are possible (except for the swim and I'll tell you about that one later) while on a passage. I love to cook, so I spent the better part of the day preparing gourmet meals. This is not easy in lumpy, bumpy seas when it is

121

difficult to stand upright, let alone balance pots and pans. Balanced meals took on a whole new meaning. Many of our meals ended up on the floor before reaching our stomachs. Foul language was the new dialect from the galley. The more I complained, the more entertained Steve was. The SSB and ham radio became my best friends as I could talk with someone else besides Steve. I was having an affair with the radio. I couldn't wait until radio net time. There were two in the morning and one at night. I couldn't get enough of it. The other thing I couldn't get enough of was sleep. Someone has always got to be on watch and lookout for ships and other nasty items in the sea, so we take turns all night with three hour shifts. During those times, I did enjoy looking at the stars and listening to music on my Walkman. One night I fell asleep while on watch and fell off the cockpit seat onto the floor with a terrible thump that woke Steve up from a deep sleep to find his first-mate laying flat with a bump on her head.

Another day when there wasn't any wind and we were drifting on the beautiful blue, glassy sea, I decided I wanted to go for a swim. We have done this before so I was not afraid. Steve dragged a rope behind the boat for us to hold on to. He instructed me to go in first and he would jump in later. I had no sooner gotten wet than the wind picked up and continued to increase. I was holding onto the rope for dear life and felt like a fish being dragged through the water. I had my exercise for the day getting back aboard. Steve had his entertainment at my expense. And so, day after day we eat, listen to the radio nets, nap, prepare a meal, eat, sail change, plot our course, eat again, talk on another net, sail change, nap, read to each other, nap and take watch and email—day after day after day—twenty-eight long days.

Steve's Trip
The passage from the Galapagos to French Polynesia is the longest leg of most world cruising plans, 3,200 nautical miles. This is a marathon trip especially for a boat our size with a max hull speed of about 6.5 knots. It is not a race, but it is a great test of our skill and endurance. It is also a test of the boat, its systems and

122

rigging. Twenty-eight days of continuous hard sailing is more than many boats see in years of use back home. I love sailing in strong winds, it seems like that's what a sailboat was built to do. It's a great challenge to get the sails trimmed right so the boat is balanced to sail herself with just the wind-vane steering her. A sailboat is an amazing piece of machinery when everything is working in harmony and she can sail herself hands off for hours or even days at a time. Even when we are sailing hard and crashing through twenty-foot waves and the boat is balanced, I can go below and sleep easy while Sharon is on watch. So for me, time went fast. This passage was one of the highlights of our continuing adventure.

Sharon
The best part of any passage for me is landfall. Making landfall on Fatu Hiva in the Marquesas, French Polynesia, was a most gratifying event! On Saturday May 4th 2002 we arrived on Fatu Hiva, the most beautiful island I have ever seen. We anchored in the Bay of Penises—no joke! Jutting over a thousand feet in the air are giant towering semi-hard shafts of warm rock that shoved up vertically into the air during a volcanic eruption. The bay is surrounded with razor sharp serrated edges by these step pinnacle rocks. The color is lush green set amid a azure sea of blue. There are palm trees everywhere, even on the high cliffs, bending and swaying in the breeze. Behind all this is a stunning two-hundred-foot waterfall. It is so achingly beautiful I wanted to cry. Sunny Polynesian magic is in the air. I thought I was in a mystical place of rare beauty.

When we sailed into the anchorage, twenty other cruising boats from all over the world blasting their horns in welcome greeted us. Fellow cruisers who rowed their dinghy to our boat and presented us with fresh baked French bread and grapefruit welcomed us.

After almost three years of Spanish speaking countries, we are at a loss for words, as the language here is French or Tahitian. The village of about two-hundred is charming. The natives are famous for their many graceful outrigger canoes that are used for fishing. There is no bank or stores, so the natives are really into trading. A t-shirt will get you all the fruit you can carry. The women especially like nail polish and perfume. By the time most cruisers reach the Marquises, they are out of eggs. Everyone was asking where to get eggs. One lady came up to me and asked, "Do you have perfume?" I said yes, and she said she had eggs. The next day I went to her home, perfume in hand, for my trade. We went to the chicken nest and picked out eight fresh eggs. The egg lady smiled at her perfume, I went back to my boat to decide what to make with my eggs. Steve and I had quite a discussion as to what to make with the eggs. We could use all of them in an omelet or use some in brownies and have a few for French toast in the morning. Brownies and French toast won out. As I cracked open my first "fresh" egg, out came a baby chick embryo. I screamed and Steve said it was an extra bonus and was good to eat. I threw it out, cracked the second "fresh" egg with the same result. We ended up with four eggs with embryos and four without, so we got our brownies but no French toast. I wanted my perfume back. Steve says that's how they eat their eggs here, but I'm not so sure.

There is a bakery (a little hut with a stone oven) that bakes the best French bread I have ever eaten. While we were there, the village had a pig-roast and invited all the boats anchored in the harbor - about twenty of us representing twelve different countries. One of the local girls was celebrating her birthday that day and the cruisers sang *Happy Birthday* in twelve different languages (one at a time). It gave me goose bumps. No problem with World Peace here. There was traditional drumming and some dancing. I had a lesson in Tahitian hip shaking.

After about two weeks of rest on Fatu Hiva, we sailed over to Tahuata, a small island with crystal clear water and a white sandy beach. There were about ten other boats anchored there where we met up with friends on S/V *Herron's Flight*, who we hadn't seen since Mexico over one and a half years ago. What a nice reunion. I celebrated my 56th birthday here with ten other boats in a dinghy raft-up. I had *Happy Birthday* sung to me in about nine different languages. That night we all saw the green-flash, which is an actual green color flash just before the sun sinks into the horizon. It is seldom seen, but is beautiful. This was my first time seeing it. Just as everyone was singing *Happy Birthday* and the sun was setting, the green flash appeared with everyone cheering. We had a beautiful crimson sunset. What a wonderful birthday gift.

After about ten days of swimming, snorkeling and visiting, it was time to see a big town. We sailed to the island of Hiva Oa to anchor in the bay near the town of Atuona. It was a beautiful island with lush mountains and flowers everywhere. The entire island smells like gardenias. I loved it! All the women (and many men) wear flowers in their hair and leis around their neck. It's what Hawaii must have been like one hundred years ago. The big town of Atuona has three stores, a bank, a hospital, two restaurants and 1,500 very friendly locals. We have found that everywhere in French Polynesia, the natives are extremely friendly and go out of their way to help you.

Steve
The Polynesian people are some of the friendliest generous folks on earth. Most are very happy but some think they would be happier if they were independent from France; some are unhappy with French and U.S. nuclear testing here. A number of them suffer the side effects of radiation poisoning, but the French refuse to acknowledge that. The French have tight control here and by pumping a lot of money in, they subsidize the native's standard of living. Therefore, we don't expect to see any big move for independence for a long time. These people have a good life without having to work too hard for it.

Sharon
Everything in French Polynesia is very expensive except for trading. After coming from Ecuador, where everything is so cheap, this is a shock. We were warned ahead of time, but still not prepared. Fuel is $5 a gallon (it was under $1 in Ecuador). Propane for cooking is

$21 for a twenty pound bottle ($1.50 in Ecuador). A half-gallon bottle of bleach is $7. It's a good thing we stocked up in Panama.

While we were at Hiva Oa, they put on a traditional Tahitian and Marquesan dance event and all the cruisers were invited. The chief sent the local school bus to pick us all up. When we arrived it was dark and we walked through a path lit by tiki torches and were welcomed by grass skirted, tattooed native men with spears. I thought I had gone back a hundred years in time. The dancing was as graceful and beautiful as the young girls. The drumming and chanting vibrated through the night and I realized this is why I came cruising. What an unbelievable experience.

We had a four-day passage from the Marquesas to the Tua-motus. How very different these islands are. The groups of islands are actually coral atolls. Tuamotus means "low and dangerous archipelago" because reefs surround the islands. The only means to the island is through a pass in the reef at slack water (between high and low tide). There are a number of yachts lost on reefs each year so it is more difficult sailing, but well worth it. The islands are very flat, white sand beaches and palm trees (just like postcards showing deserted islands). This is also the area where the cultured black pearls are harvested. Japan has played a part in helping with this industry. A good black pearl is said to be worth $100 - $1,000. While on the island of Raroia, we visited a family-run pearl farm and became friends with the family. I was able to trade a bottle of whisky that our exchange daughter from Japan had given us for nine beautiful pearls. I will have them set for our daughters.

Steve
One night while anchored off the village at Raroia, we had a squall come in with high winds. We dragged anchor in the middle of the night and woke up to do a Chinese fire drill. It was about mid-night on a moonless, pitch-black night. Before we could get the engine started the tiller was jerked out of my hand as our rudder crashed into a coral head on the reef. We started the engine and tried to pull ahead but we were stuck. We put out a *May Day* call on the

126

radio and our friends on S/V *White Hawk* nearby answered the call and launched their dinghy to come help us. With our friends help, we pulled up the anchor and maneuvered to deeper water and reset the anchor. After checking the bilge to make sure we were not taking on water, we settled back to sleep.

Next day, we found that the main keel and rudder were fine but the wind vane steering rudder was badly bent. We managed to pull the bent shaft (one and a half inch stainless steel pipe nine feet long) out and took it in to the village dock. We looked for a big pipe to use for a lever to straighten the shaft, but the small village didn't have much in the way of tools. So we gave up for the day and left the shaft on the dock.

The next morning I went back to the dock to work on it, but discovered that it had already been straightened. Apparently, the men in the village had fixed it. They asked for nothing in return, but we gave them some small gifts and some food.

Sharon

Ciguatera is a fish poisoning from eating fish caught near coral atolls in parts of French Polynesia. Many of the islands are affected by it, but on the island of Makemo there is no ciguatera so you can eat any of the fish. So we were off to Makemo. We anchored off the village of Makemo. The day we arrived there was a wedding and all the cruisers were invited to the wedding feast. It was very beautiful and interesting with a procession through the village to the church. The most interesting part was the feast after the ceremony. Along with rice, coconut and breadfruit dishes, the main course was roast pig, goat and dog. Yes, you read that correctly - DOG. Since I am a seafood vegetarian, I passed, but most of the men ate it, and the next day I think they were barking.

After a few days at this village, we sailed twelve miles east to do some of the best snorkeling and diving we have ever done. The colors of the coral were unbelievable; red, purple, pink, blue and orange. It was like visiting an underwater garden. And the fish were

127

equally beautiful in color. The visibility was one-hundred-fifty feet. I felt like we were anchored on a piece of turquoise blue glass. It was incredible! There were eight boats moored. Every night we had potluck dinners or watched videos on someone's boat. The spear fishing was great; we dined on fish, lobster and scallops. It doesn't get much better than this. It's like playing Robinson Caruso with friends.

The downside of Makemo was the sharks that appeared when you speared a fish. They would appear and circle you as soon as the gun went off. My job was to fend them off with the Hawaiian sling until Steve got the fish into the dinghy. This job does not pay enough. One day Steve caught an eighty pound shark and hung it from our boat, which caused much talk in the anchorage. He then cut it up, cooked and ate it. I much prefer grouper. It was time to leave when we ran out of fresh fruits and veggies. We needed a city fix and so we were off to Tahiti, 350 miles southwest. We had an uneventful passage to Tahiti, anchoring with about one-hundred boats from all over the world. We ran into people we hadn't seen since Mexico and Central America. It was like a convention of cruisers. We really enjoyed Tahiti. The scenery is spectacular, the water crystal clear and the dancing, drumming and singing is sensational. It is however, expensive. I use to say that someday I would be doing laundry in a bucket in Tahiti and enjoying it. And here I am!

We were hoping to fly home for a visit, but for many reasons involving the French bureaucracy, that did not work out. We will continue west to Bora Bora, then the Cook Islands and Tonga. We may spend Cyclone season in New Zealand and fly home from there. More long passages.

What Is A Family?

Sharon Reed-Hendricks

What is a family? What is a home?
It's that warm special feeling that you're not alone
It's support when you need it - unconditional love
It's a shelter that's more than the roof up above

It's the sharing you feel and the sharing you give
It's a full time commitment - you're willing to live
It's not that it's yours and it's not that it's mine
But together it's ours, for all of life's time

It's being a unit - together we're strong
It matters so little if we're right or we're wrong
It's knowing the other is there and will stay
No matter what happens, they won't go away

It's knowing you need them and that they are there
They're always supportive because they do care
It's the time that they give just to be there with you
It's that wonderful feeling that we're one and not two

10   Tahiti and the Cook Islands

Sharon

We loved Tahiti for its beautiful scenery, clear water and exotic dancing, but it is one of the most expensive places I have ever been to. I think they even charge you to breathe the air there! Produce was unbelievably expensive, but you could get everything and anything, for a price. One thing that was a bargain was the French baguettes. They cost 30 cents and we ate several loaves every day. With all this great food, we just had to have a cruisers potluck. So I helped organize one of the biggest and best potlucks we have ever seen with about 200 cruisers. We also had some great entertainment as many of the cruisers play musical instruments. What fun!

While anchored in Tahiti, some of the cruisers knew I cut hair and had always cut Steve's, so word went around the anchorage and soon several cruisers asked if I would cut their hair. I made an announcement on the local net that I would be available one day on the dock and payment could be in trade—I needed fruits and veggies. For the next two days I was very busy cutting hair and bringing home tons of fruit and veggies, so by day three, I changed the fee to paper towels and toilet paper. With all that fruit you make more trips to the bathroom. It's nice to have a useful talent, even though it has been years since I did it professionally. I had great fun, met lots of new cruisers, and didn't have to shop for produce for weeks.

When I visit a new country I always inquire about AA meetings. In Tahiti I was given a phone number of a French official to contact. When I called, the man on the phone spoke English, which really helped. I was told there was a meeting that evening and the man on the phone would pick me up and drive me to the meeting in town. He also was a member of AA.

That evening Steve rowed me to the dock where I waited alone in the dark for a French man I didn't even know, in a country where I didn't speak the language, to pick me up and take me to a meeting. Boy am I trusting—or stupid. Anyway, he arrived and drove me to the meeting where they had a translator (a good looking Frenchman) who sat next to me and translated the entire meeting to me. It was a most memorable meeting and I met the most interesting people.

Every July Tahiti celebrates Bastille Days, a festival of traditional Tahitian arts and crafts along with competitive events from every island group. Events such as canoe races, javelin throwing, fire walking, fruit carriers and song and dance competitions are going on every day of the month. We were privileged to be there during that time. This was another experience of a lifetime. We got tickets to the dance competition in the open-air theater one evening and what a show! The Polynesian dancing was outstanding. Both the girls and the guys could really shake those hips. The costumes out did any Las Vegas performance you have ever seen. It was an unbelievable night we will never forget.

As we traveled from island group to island group, I never tired of the Polynesian dancing. We saw many groups perform on many islands and each was a unique experience. The ones I really enjoyed the most were the kids; the little girls of five and six years old who could shake those hips better than the adults. I think they're born moving those hips. I had a few lessons and I think I might have the hang of it but the grass skirt keeps falling off when the hips move. I don't know how they keep them on.

The island of Moorea is only a few hour sail from Tahiti yet it seemed to represent more of my idea of a Polynesian island. It is breathtaking to be anchored in Robinson's Cove with a view of Mount Tohieva and the spire of Mount Mouaroa in the background. This was the backdrop in the movie *South Pacific* and it is drop-dead beautiful! In my opinion, Moorea was more beautiful and a little less expensive than Tahiti or Bora Bora. We spent a few weeks enjoying the water, walking and hiking the island. We took in a few local dance shows at the famous thatched-roof bungalow of the Bali Hai Hotel. I could have stayed here forever, but to do that one needs a lot of money or to be a native and subsidized by the French Government.

Bora Bora is another beautiful island paradise, however I think it is over rated. There are too many tourists and prices higher than Tahiti, if you can believe that. It gets such great publicity that everyone thinks it's the most beautiful island in the world. And it probably is if you have nothing else to compare it with. The island itself is lovely and the turquoise water surrounding it is exquisite and we enjoyed some great snorkeling. However, it is not one of my favorite islands, but it is nice to say you have been to Bora Bora.

It was now August and we were starting our fourth year of cruising. It is also time to say goodbye to French Polynesia and many cruising friends who are going in other directions. As if I needed a reminder of three years ago, when with tears in our eyes, we said goodbye to many cruising friends and headed out on what seemed to be a "nice" passage. The first day or so was calm with gentle breezes and then on Steve's birthday, August 2nd, the winds and seas started to build. I wanted to make a special birthday dinner but that was quickly canceled when the wind built to 40 knots and the seas were confused and big. This is the price we pay to visit these beautiful islands. Sometimes it is too expensive a price for me. Along with all this wind and big seas, we had driving rain. The temperature dropped to 67 degrees. This may not seem cold to you, but when you are used to 80 plus, 67 degrees can feel very cold and I was miserable. Steve didn't like it either, but unlike me, he slept like a baby while I was on watch. The storm lasted for five long, cold, uncomfortable, miserable days. Everything below in our cabin was wet and scattered, including me. I was sick and tired of cruising, sick of the weather, sick of Steve and sick of everything. Finally, on day eight, we arrived on the island of Rarotonga in the Cook Islands, one of the most beautiful islands in the South Pacific and maybe my new home. I wanted to apply for citizenship because I wasn't going out on that ocean again— at least not for a while.

It wasn't just the passage, even if I had arrived by plane I would have fallen in love with this island. I really could live here. There are many beautiful islands in the South Pacific, but I'm not sure I would want to live for very long at any of them—until Rarotonga. The island has a history, beauty and magic to rival Hawaii and Tahiti. Unlike those Polynesian islands, however, the world has virtually passed it by. It is a spectacular, mountainous island fringed by a coral reef. There is an International Airport (not busy at all) and several island resorts. The Cook Islands are linked to New Zealand as they have New Zealand citizenship and use New Zealand currency ($1US = $2NZ at that time). Prices are much better here than French Polynesia. In fact we found it to be one of the cheapest in all the South Pacific so far. I was able to get my black pearls set into beautiful necklaces here for half the price of Tahiti and they did a beautiful job.

The people here speak English with a New Zealand accent. After three years in Spanish speaking countries, this was very different for us. The people in the Cook Islands are the friendliest we have ever met anywhere so far. Everyone is so helpful and interested in where you have come from. The main mode of transportation here is motor scooter and everyone just leaves the key in the ignition. This is one of the safest places we have ever been. Raro, as the locals call it, has several good restaurants, a couple of great super markets, hardware stores and pharmacy's, all with New Zealand products. They also have a great hospital. The downtown is located on the waterfront and reminds me of a small California coastal town with fewer tourists; it's very Polynesian (like Hawaii). Everyone walks around with lei's around their neck or flowers in their hair. Flowers are everywhere. There is a great outdoor produce market right next to the harbor where we could get almost anything at very good prices.

Dancing in the Cook Islands is spectacular. The Cook Islanders are reputed to be the best in Polynesia, even better than the Tahitians.

The dancing is often suggestive and the men are as suggestive as the women. One evening the cruisers went out to dinner where a special dance group from another island was entertaining. What a show! The best part was the show after the show, when the dancers came to the tables and picked partners from the audience to dance with them on the stage. And guess what—you guessed right—one of the muscular young men picked me. How embarrassing! But what fun.

We rented a motor scooter for a week here for the same price they wanted for a day in French Polynesia. Steve had to get a Cook Island driver's license and take a driving test on the scooter. This may sound easy but they drive on the left side of the road here. He passed only because he followed a guy from New Zealand in front of him who was also taking the test. For two dollars he now has a Cook Island driver's license complete with a picture and good for one year. It was a good thing he had me for a back seat driver yelling in his ear "left side—left side," as he often reverted back to the right side of the road. We had great fun exploring all the back roads of this lush and beautiful island. I fell more in love with it every day. The weather was great. It was in the 70's day and night. We got to know the man and his wife that Steve followed during his driver's test. They were in Raro on holiday from New Zealand. Since we all hit it off so well, they invited us to their condo on the beach for dinner. They have a catering business in New Zealand so they prepared us a great dinner. We had them out to our boat and they invited us to visit with them again when we get to New Zealand. The best part of cruising is always the people you meet.

If you ever visit Rarotonga, and I highly recommend it, be sure to go to church to hear the singing. It's outstanding! The dancing and the singing alone are worth the trip. Of course I love everything about this place and I wish I could settle here, but we are cruisers and the harbor here is not safe for a boat during the cyclone season. I guess I will have to come back another time. And I will. We had to move on. We were headed to Palmerston Island, a very remote atoll about 350 miles northwest of Rarotonga.

Since Palmerston only gets a supply ship every three to six months, we were told to put out the word in Raro to relatives living here so they can send things via our sailboat and have us deliver supplies to their isolated relatives. A supply ship left Raro for Palmerston just weeks before we left so we were not as loaded down as we could have been. We sadly left, Rarotonga and had a rough three-day passage to Palmerston.

Palmerston Atoll—Population: 72
Palmerston Island is a bit of a Cook Island oddity. William Marsters, legendary prolific settler, arrived here in 1862, bringing with him his three Polynesian wives. By the time he died at the age of seventy-eight, he had begotten somewhere between twenty-six and sixty children, depending on who you talk too. We also learned he had three plus one wife. It seems his friend, a Spanish explorer, also lived on this island with his wife. When the Spanish friend went back to Spain, Marsters took over his wife too. All of the inhabitants of Palmerston are descendants of William Marsters. He had strict rules regarding intermarriages, so many Marsters go to other islands to find partners to bring back to Palmerston. Many of his descendants control the island while the rest live in New Zealand and other Cook Islands such as Rarotonga. William Marsters is buried next to the church on Palmerston.

The island is divided into three sections for each of the three families. The three branches of the family live in a perpetual state of feud. We could never figure out where the dividing lines were, but they sure knew! The island itself is just beautiful, with very clear water, white sand beaches and swaying coconut palms. The picture perfect South Pacific Island. We had whales, turtles and dolphins visit our boat daily.

Upon dropping anchor on this idyllic island, you are immediately greeted by a skiff full of locals. They welcome you to their island and come aboard to chat. They will invite you to dinner and will return to pick you up later in the afternoon and taxi you through the treacherous reef to their home.

You are then "adopted" or "owned" by that family for the remainder of your stay. They actually fight over which family adopts you. One is expected to have lunch and dinner with their host family every-day and join in their activities. They ask for nothing in return, but they do accept gifts and loved it when Steve fixed several items for them. Once you are adopted by a family branch you are not sup-posed to mix with the other family branches. Each family branch consists of about four or five families. Since I like to visit and talk with everyone, I soon got into trouble by accepting a lunch invitation from another family branch. I also ask them to do my laundry (another no-no). I had a lot of fast-talking to do to get myself out of that one.

We visited the one-room schoolhouse and talked with the schoolmaster Kevin, a young man from England. I did a poetry class with the children and donated one of my books to the school. Some of the children shared poetry they had written and we touched each other's hearts. Kevin has a tough job as he has all the children from all three branches of the families and can't show any favoritism. He explained that this adoption process has been going on for years and sometimes it's the only contact from the outside world these people have. The three family branches do co-operate every evening (except Sunday) in a competitive game of volleyball. Steve and I joined in a couple of games but these folks are pros. Six nights a week means you're good. Sunday is strictly observed, no work - no play. On that day they only go to church and eat. The food is cooked in an underground oven on Sunday. No fishing, no swimming, no game playing. It's a very quiet day. Men must wear shirts and women wear dresses or skirts.

The families also cooperate on a sea bird hunt activity. We hap-pened to be there during this annual event. Actually, Steve went and I stayed behind to show some of the women how to make piz-zas.

Steve

137

The natives took me on a wild bird hunt on a remote island across the lagoon at Plamerston. We chased around through the bushes and caught about one-hundred white baby Sea Turns, too young to fly yet. They were about six weeks old (about the size of a small fryer chicken). When we got back to the village we put all the birds in a pen on the beach. With the whole village looking on, the birds were carefully divided up amongst the families. We rung their necks and plucked the big feathers. Then the birds were placed on a stick and the fuzzy feathers were burned off over an open fire. The next morning the birds were placed in an underground oven called an umu and baked until well done. A bit gamey tasting, but out here where they don't see a supply boat for a year sometimes, any meat besides fish is a welcome addition to the table.

Sharon

We ate these birds for Sunday dinner. Being the honest person I am, I told my family I really didn't like the taste of the bird (it was awful) so I was excused from eating it. Steve on the other hand, trying to be polite, said he liked it (he lies) so they gave him two birds to eat. It pays to be honest.

It was with mixed feelings that we left Palmerston for the unbelievable island of Niue. We had a rough four-day passage to Niue and a night encounter with a whale. I wish I could enjoy these passages as much as Steve.

Steve

It was a magnificent star filled night on a passage to Niue with a nice fifteen knot wind pushing us along at 6 knots. I was on watch relaxing in the cockpit about midnight, when all of a sudden the ocean next to me explodes in a loud geyser of water and air as a whale exhales eight feet from where I was sitting. I jump up and saw the glistening dorsal fin of giant a humpback whale swimming alongside of us. He slipped back below the surface and I said to myself, "Wow, that was close!" Five minutes later as I begin to relax, again the water explodes in another twenty five foot geyser.

138

This whale proceeds to follow right next to us (ten to fifty feet away). For the next three hours, every five minutes when he exhales, the water explodes out of his back in a geyser like somebody knocked over a fire hydrant. This made me very nervous because I could not see him very well in the dark and I know of other whales that behaved in this manner and eventually turned to ram and sink the sailboats they were swimming with. Being worried about what could happen, I woke up Sharon to help watch and be prepared for a collision. It was like sailing with a big submarine next to us. As we surfed through ten foot breaking seas he stayed right with us. I tried running our motor and turning on lights to see if that would discourage him from following but that seemed to have no effect on him. Then I noticed when the boat turned a little north he came even closer and his breathing seemed more forced and irritated with us. I slowly turned the boat south and after three long hours he eventually left us. We love seeing whales, but not that close and not at night. Maybe he/she was protecting a calf nearby. Or maybe it was mating season.

Sharon
Niue is one of the world's smallest self-governing countries, in association with New Zealand. They also use New Zealand currency. About ten-thousand Niueans live in New Zealand and every year more people leave to seek employment there. You'll never see as many empty houses and near-ghost towns as here. You can buy a house for next to nothing (I almost did) but there is little work to be had. If you're retired and love adventure this is the place.

This little known island boasts the finest coastal limestone crevices and chasms in the South Pacific. Niue is for the explorer and is one of the most unspoiled islands in the Pacific. It's an island of adventure. The water is the clearest I have seen, with visibility to two-hundred feet and countless species of colorful fish. Butterflies, birds and flowers are everywhere. I don't know how to begin to tell you how beautiful and unique this island is. Because it is in the cyclone path, one cannot leave a boat here safely during cyclone season; otherwise I would have stayed forever and made this my home. We rented motorcycles for a week to tour the island and explore its spectacular caves. Each day we would hike into a cave or chasm and swim in the crystal clear pools. We visited villages and talked with the people. One day we met the Prime Minister and the Vice Prime Minister. I got along great with the Vice Prime Minister, as we are both writers. She invited me to join her for lunch at the festival that weekend. We also visited the honey factory and bought some of the best honey I have ever tasted. Niue is famous for its honey.

Niue has a small but adequate market on Tuesdays and Saturdays. However, I was told the best and freshest place to get your produce was the prison. After several locals insisted that was the best place, we decided to give it a try. It's hard to believe that Niue actually has a prison and they had three prisoners, all of them in for murder. We needed directions, as there was no indication that it was a prison. It looked like a cute little yellow house surrounded by three of the most beautiful gardens I had ever seen. It was down the road from the honey factory and next to a golf course. There were no bars or locks anywhere. There was a little gate that was open and I walked through and look around until I found someone in the garden. A smiling prisoner greeted me with a big knife in his hand that he used to cut the vegetables.

Steve toured and talked with one of the prisoners as I cut vegetables with the other. I had so much produce it filled a big box all for only five dollars. We had quite a talk in the garden. It seems the prisoner killed his mother-in-law. Later we found most of the town couldn't blame him. The one Steve talked with was a prison guard but shot one of the prisoners in self-defense. We found out later he shot him in the back three times. We're not sure of the third one's story. When I asked one of the men how long he was in for and he said maybe seven years but, "It's not such a bad life. It's not like we're locked away or anything. We do our own cooking, our family visits anytime and we play golf three times a week." I don't know when I've had such an interesting morning buying produce. I could go on and on about Niue but it would fill another book. I will come back someday as three weeks is not near long enough.

I'll Give You The World

Sharon Reed-Hendricks

I can give you gifts my child
And I can give you toys
I can give you all those things
Parents give to girls and boys

But I can give you so much more
If you will know its worth
I can give you all the world
And everything on earth

Everything you'll ever need
Is here - but not in stores
If you follow all your dreams
You'll find that it is yours

And only you will have the answers
For you alone will know
What you want and what you need
And just where you must go

All you have to do is go
To find out what you need
Search the whole world till you find
The life that you must lead

11   The Kingdom of Tonga

Sharon

We had a three-day passage from Niue to Tonga and arrived in the Vava'u group of Tonga on the 13th of September, but it was actually the 14th. You see, we crossed the International Date Line, so we lost a day. Friday the 13th is a good day to lose. When you are in this part of the world you are one day ahead of the States. So when it's Friday in the States, it's Saturday in this part of the world. The day begins in Tonga.

Polynesia's oldest and last remaining monarchy, the Kingdom of Tonga, consists of 170 or so remarkably diverse islands. It's located about four-hundred miles southeast of Fiji and 1,100 miles northeast of New Zealand. Tonga is divided into three main parts; the Tongatapu Group in the south, with the capital of Nuku'alofa where the King and Royal Palace are located; the Ha'apai Group, a far-flung archipelago of low coral islands, much like the Tuamotus in French Polynesia with soaring volcanoes in the center; the Vava'u Group in the north with its immense landlocked harbor and beautiful close-together islands only a day's sail apart. We visited all three island groups and thoroughly enjoyed them all.

The people of Tonga speak a Polynesian variant called Tongan, but most (not all) speak some English. The people are friendly but a little shy, and are very big people. I think it's the coconut cream. To a Tongan, great physical size is a measure of beauty and I at one-hundred pounds was not so attractive. Tongan women begin increasing prodigiously in beauty from about the age of thirteen onward. So guys, if you want a shapely Tonga girlfriend you got to get 'em really young. They also wear very strange clothes. The ta' ovala is the distinctive Tongan skirt and is worn by both men and women. Made of a finely woven pandanus-leaf mat, it is worn around the waist. These mats are often prized heirlooms. The sight of a group of large Tongan women on the road, each with a huge mat tied around them, is truly striking. Steve says it looks like they are wearing the living room carpet. They are large enough people anyway, and to add these huge mats makes the women appear even larger. This is one traditional outfit I chose not to purchase. The thought of wearing a mat the size of a living room carpet in the heat of Tonga would have me lying in the street from heat exhaustion.

In Tonga, women must have their shoulders covered as well as their legs, at least to the knee. This applies to visitors as well as locals. Very few Tongans have bathing suits, they just jump into the water with whatever they have on. Every Tongan family has pigs, not just a pig, but several, and they have the run of the town. You can't walk a block without tripping over a pig, or a litter of piglets. I didn't see too many dogs, but saw more pigs than I've ever seen in my life (helps to fatten up the girls). Tongan food is different with lots of taro (a root vegetable), pork, seafood, and tropical fruit and of course coconut cream on everything. The produce at the market place was inexpensive and good.

One could spend years in Tonga and never see it all. The Vava'u Group is a sailor's paradise consisting of about fifty tranquil islands, all within a day's sail of each other. After nine-thousand nautical miles of passage across the Pacific, it seemed like heaven to be in these islands and day sail only. The islands consist of numerous sea caves, beautiful sandy beaches, underwater coral gardens in crystal clear water and well protected anchorages.

In the main town of Neiafu, we anchored amongst one-hundred other cruisers from all over the world, some we had not seen in months, or even years. Again, it was like a big reunion. Ana's Cafe was the main cruisers' hangout with its large dinghy dock and many activities and meals. While in Neiafu, a local man was bit by a tiger shark while on a whale watch swim (this rarely happens). He nearly lost his leg and was sent to Nuku'alofa to hospital. Ana's Cafe and all the cruisers held a fundraiser to help with the bills. I did haircuts and raised three-hundred dollars. After the fundraiser I was still busy cutting hair and made a few dollars for our cruising fund plus many new friends.

It's difficult to leave the activities of Neiafu and sail the islands, but it's only a day sail from island to island so it's easy to cruise the islands and return to Neiafu when you need to stock up. The islands are beautiful and the snorkeling is superb. The Moorings Charter Service runs boats out of here so they have re-named the islands by number rather than the difficult Tongan name. So the cruisers also referred to the anchorages by numbers. Number 7 was my favorite, but number 16 had the best snorkeling and shell collecting. Between anchorage number 7 and 8 is a little village that holds a Tongan feast every Saturday night with heaps of local Tongan food including roast pig, lobster and more fruits and veggies than you could imagine plus local dancing. We attended the feast with about ten other cruisers and had the experience of a lifetime. All the food was grown or harvested from the little island and we ate with our fingers on plates of banana leaves. Huge clam-shells were used as serving bowls. Everything was biodegradable - and no dishes to wash. That's the way it should be done. No waste.

Tongan is known for its basket weaving and woodcarving and every village has its craftsman; beautiful baskets and wood-carvings are everywhere. Usually they come to you. Steve called them the traveling basket salesmen. They row their dugout canoe out to your boat and before you know it they are seated in your cockpit with a big smile and a basket full of products. It's fun to bargain with them. They even like to trade, which is my favorite past time. Steve says, by the time they leave our boat, they owe me. You have to watch those big ladies though. If there is more than one, you need to sit them on opposite sides of the boat for balance. No kidding, these women weigh in at about four-hundred pounds. We have so many baskets and woodcarvings on board I'm not sure we can carry them all home on the airplane when we go to visit.

We also happened to be in Neiafu for two special events. One was the dedication of the newly built school, which was destroyed by the hurricane last January. The King arrived and there was a big

145

feast and all were invited. There was dancing and feasting all day. The other event was the craft festival and the princess was there for this one (boy is she big). She got all her crafts free while the rest of us had to pay or trade.

I was asked to read my poetry to the children of Neiafu one Saturday at the local library. What an awesome experience. There were about seventy-five children and they love to be read to in English by someone who speaks it as their first language. After I read, they shared their poetry in Tongan and then we sang, *I'm a Little Teapot* and *Itsy, Bitsy Spider* in English and Tongan. I can now say my poetry is going international.

Between anchorage number 7 and anchorage number 9 are two famous and interesting caves. One is Swallows Cave into which one can take a dinghy and the other is Mariner's Cave. We packed a picnic and spent a day exploring and snorkeling Swallows Cave by dinghy with another couple. It is a fascinating cave. Next to it is a smaller and even more beautiful cave. The next day five couples got together and sailed the largest boat, which was a fifty foot Catamaran to Mariner's Cave. Mariner's Cave is a hidden underwater cave requiring good snorkeling skills to enter. Will Mariner was apparently the first European to see it. Mariner was puzzled when he saw several chiefs dive into the water and not return to the surface. He was then instructed to follow their example and was guided into a three meter-long channel, a meter or so below the surface of the water. When you emerge, you are in a dim cathedral-like cavern. The cavern is about fourteen meters high and fourteen meters wide. Once inside the cave, you experience the strange atmospheric phenomenon that occurs there. Pacific swells surging through the entrance compresses trapped air, condensing it into a heavy green fog every few seconds. As the sea recedes the fog vanishes—another awesome experience!

The history behind the cave tells of a young Tongan Chief who, fell in love with a beautiful maiden of a family who was due for extermination in the civic broils of the time. They took her away

146

from danger, and hid her for two weeks in the cave.

With the help of a couple of my scuba diving friends to hold my floating body downward, I made it into the cave. You have to dive down about three feet and then swim underwater for about twelve feet before entering the cave. I did it but with a little help.

Steve

The Polynesian's are very talented when it comes to art and music. So we were surprised when we heard the high school band practicing and they sounded awful—off key and out of tune. Our friends Neal and Nancy, who happen to be professional musicians, decided to go see if they could somehow help the band. What they found were the kids doing their best playing very old instruments that were in terrible condition. All the band instruments belong to the school and have been used for many years by hundreds of kids. The school could not afford new brass horns as they have many more pressing needs like classrooms and desks. The day I went to the high school, the boys were mixing concrete by hand and pouring a foundation for a new classroom. That night we got together with Neil and Nancy for dinner. Neil was telling me how appalled he was at the condition of the band equipment. I told him, I am no musician since getting kicked out of band in the sixth grade. However, I am pretty good at fixing things and maybe I could fix some of the plumbing in those old brass horns. He said he had no experience with that, but it would be worth a try.

The next morning I loaded up my tool bag, along with all my soldering and brazing equipment and we set out for the school. The band director was skeptical that we could do anything. The instruments had been in this condition since he was in high school ten years ago and he accepted this as normal. The horns were crumpled, bent, cracked and many of the moving parts froze-up. Parts and pieces were literally held together with bailing wire and chewing gum. We picked out some of the worst horns first and started working on knocking the dents out and soldering them back together. Many had cracks and holes that made them near impossible to play. Some were broke in two pieces and the kids had to hold them together while they tried to play. At the end of the day we had fixed four trumpets, three trombones and one tuba.

The next day we heard the band classes practicing and they sounded a lot better from a distance. That afternoon we went into the village and ran into the band director. He was grinning from ear to ear and said he could not believe the difference we made in the sound of his band classes. The kids were doing fair with bad instruments but now they were able to make beautiful music with horns that worked.

Sharon

It was peer pressure—that's the only excuse I have. All the other ladies got tattoos in French Polynesia and I didn't. I said that I would never get a tattoo (also said I would never live on a boat) and then I was sorry that I didn't get one. So there I was in Tonga, complaining that I didn't have a tattoo, when a local Tongan artist who works at our friend's T-shirt shop mentioned that her cousin was a tattoo artist. Well, that's all it took and I was off to the local tattoo hut with four other ladies to hold my hand and hold me down. Steve didn't even want to take part in this ritual. I don't remember if I screamed too loud, but I do remember the tattoo artist's old grandmother hiding behind the curtain in the hut. She peeked out from time to time with her eyes shut and a painful look on her face. Two hours later, with tears in my eyes, I emerged with a beautiful little green, red and black Gecko (lizard) on my left ankle crawling up my leg. All I can say is, it hurt like hell and I will never do that again.

After about five weeks in the Vava'u Group, which was not long enough, we decided to head south to the seldom visited islands of the Ha'apai Group with the idea of going to New Zealand. An over-night sail had us anchored by morning in the beautiful islands of the Ha'apai Group which are characterized by low palm covered islands, long sandy beaches, beautiful coral reefs, clear water and small rural communities. We had a relaxing time walking the beautiful beaches, collecting seashells, visiting the local laid-back villages and exploring the underwater wonderland. There were only a handful of other cruisers that decided to take this less followed route, but those of us that did wouldn't have missed it for the world.

The island of Lima, a very small deserted sandy island with many coral reefs, is a snorkeler's dream. I don't know how to begin to tell you about the beauty of the coral gardens and the unique, colorful fish of this underwater paradise. Viewing the coral was like opening a box of *Crayola* crayons, with every color you can imagine and then some. The coral shapes were like big rose petals in the most beautiful shades of blues, purples, oranges, pinks, greens and reds. It was an underwater fantasy, the likes of which I have never seen. I didn't want to get out of the water and we would snorkel till I got so cold I would turn blue. We also collected some of the most magnificent shells by free diving in these waters. I never wanted to leave this place, but hurricane season was fast approaching and cruising boats needed to head to a safe haven such as New Zealand before December. We still had to sail to Nuku'alofa, the capital of Tonga, to check out of the country.

Nuku'alofa is the capital of the island of Tongatapu and is where the King resides in the palace. Nulu'alofa is a big city (well it is for Tonga) about the size of a very small town in the States. We were excited because they had restaurants and a big market, a hardware store for Steve and an ice cream store. From our anchorage we could row to shore and walk to any of these places. One day, on our walk back from town, laden with packages, I stopped for a rest in front of a wood carver's shop. The young girl there started a conversation and I was soon asking the price of some of the beautiful woodcarvings. I had no intention of buying any. She quoted me some prices of about eighty to one-hundred dollars and I said I would have to think about it. Her price kept going down and down. I really had no intention of buying, but the price was getting so low I could hardly resist. By this time I was well rested and Steve was ready to get back to the boat, so I said my goodbyes and told the young lady I would see her tomorrow. The next day, while walking into town with another cruising couple and busy talking, I had forgotten about the woodcarvings. Upon walking by the wood carver's shop, the same young girl, along with her brother, said hello and the woodcarving I was inquiring about earlier was now at a lower price; they could give it to me for twenty dollars Tongan (this is $10US). I stopped dead in my tracks and our friends couldn't believe the incredible price, nor could I. This was too good to pass up, so I asked her to hold it until I came back from town. All the way to town our friends and us talked about the unbelievable price for the beautiful woodcarving. On the way back from town Steve and I stopped at the wood carvers shop and no one was there. Looking around the corner to where the house was, I saw the wood carver himself and said I was here to pick up my woodcarving. When I pointed to the large one of the dolphins and informed him of the price, his smile turned to a look of surprise. "The young girl here this morning quoted me the price," I said. "My daughter told you twenty dollars?" asked the wood carver. When he called the young girl and her brother in, they argued in Tongan but I could guess what they were saying. When the arguing stopped, the wood carver informed me I got a very good price. I told him that's why I came back. The conversation turned to wood boats and somehow we got talking about our three-part nested wooden dinghy and next thing I knew, Victor (we were on first name basis by now) the wood carver was down at the harbor viewing our dinghy. I don't know how these things happen, but we talked about Tongan food and next thing I knew we were invited to Victor's home for dinner the next day.

What a feast—and we were honored guests. We met Victor's busy wife and fifteen children, several grandchildren and sons and daughters-in-law. I think every day is a feast at this home as there are so many people. We sat at a table with Victor while everyone else waited. We had to eat first. It's like being at a restaurant and being waited on. When we were finished, the rest of the family could eat. I don't think the mother ever sat down. Victor's wife did not speak English but one of the daughters translated for us. We talked about children and food and gardens and the fact that I look like I don't eat enough. She said she wanted me to know that anytime I come to Tonga that I have a place to stay, that I was always welcome in their home. Their home was my home. I played games with the children and brought some gifts of toys and garden seeds to the family. We had a great day. They also invited us to tour the island with them in their van the next day. What a warm and friendly family we had befriended. We found out that Victor is the master carver and has taught most of the other carvers in Tongatapu. His son and son-in-law are learning from him now. Some of Victor's carvings went to the Olympics in Utah along with Victor who presented one to the mayor. We will never forget our experience with Victor's family and hope to go back someday to visit. We now have several of Victor's woodcarvings on our boat.

With hurricane season fast approaching, we had to decide where to spend it. I was changing my mind daily as to where to go. Most cruisers were going to New Zealand but a few went to a hurricane hole in Fiji and two or three stayed in Tonga. I wanted to stay warm, but also wanted a good place to leave the boat so we could fly home. We needed a good place to haul the boat and do some work on her and it was time to have some medical check-ups. New Zealand had it all. When I finally said okay I guess I would go to New Zealand, Steve got the boat ready as fast as possible in case I changed my mind again. It was a very long eighteen-day passage. It was not fun. We had very rough seas and it got colder every day. Two of our cruising friends lost their boats on this passage, one on a reef the other hit by a ship. Both boats were lost but the people were saved. This is the stuff that really scares me.

Memories Under Our Keel

Sharon Reed-Hendricks

We shared an anchorage once or twice
And then a meal or two
We went to shore and talked some more
We really enjoyed you

As time went by we thought of you
And wondered just how far
You sailed away - and then one day
We look and there you are

Again we shared more anchorages
A swim, a walk, a meal
And all of these - sweet memories
Are now under our keel

So many friends we bid farewell
And watch them sail away
We never know - which way we'll go
And meet again someday

So we refuse to say goodbye
It's too much like an end
We'll think of you - those memories too
Until we meet again

12 New Zealand and The Bay of Islands

Sharon

After the two cruising friends lost their boats this season, I was more than a little shaken while on watch one dark night about two-hundred miles from New Zealand. Steve was fast asleep and I had just taken a good look all around the pitch black surroundings. I had gone below to pour a cup of tea (maybe five minutes, at most) and as I stepped back out into the cockpit, I was blinded by a fast approaching bright light. I quickly turned on the radar and saw a freighter about three miles away. With my heart pounding, I grabbed the VHF radio and called to the freighter. To my surprise, I received a response. Most of the time, ships are on autopilot and don't always keep a careful watch or hear a radio contact. I informed the freighter that I was the sailing vessel off his port bow and asked if he could see me, to which he responded that he did not. I stated that I was under sail and it was difficult for me to alter course. By this time Steve was awake and had turned on our bright spreader lights to illuminate our sails, to which the freighter responded that he did indeed see us now and would keep a watch out for us. By now he was only one mile away!

I can now see how quickly a freighter can appear and how our friend, who was a single handler was hit. Being alone, he had to sleep and no one was on watch at the time he was hit. We often go for weeks and never see a vessel out there, so one becomes complacent. This is a good lesson for all of us to keep a good watch, as this can happen to anyone.

When we arrived in Opua, New Zealand, Bay of Islands on the 27th of November (the day before Thanksgiving), I thought that maybe we had missed New Zealand and were in the Antarctica, it was so cold. We had come from temperatures of over 80 degrees to temperatures in the low sixty's.

Most cruising boats coming from Tonga or Fiji enter New Zealand in Opua, which is on the northern part of the North Island in the beautiful Bay of Islands. After eighteen cold, wet, and nasty days at sea, I was cold and grumpy. It looked and felt like I was back in Seattle and I really didn't want to be here. I was in no mood to deal with government officials when the customs and immigrations guys came aboard. I already knew ahead what items were not permitted to enter New Zealand; fresh fruits and veggies, dairy products and honey, popcorn, feathers, some shells (let them try to take my shells) and the list goes on and on. So this grumpy old sailor was in no mood to deal with officials. Well, they couldn't have been nicer. I think someone must have warned them about me. After a friendly big welcome to their country, they just sat down and asked, with a big smile, if I had any fresh produce after an eighteen-day passage. They didn't ask about my popcorn or dried beans and I didn't offer. They asked if I had any feathers as they looked up at my feather collection. Then they asked if the feathers came from a hat? I told them no, they came from the birds, to which they asked again if they came from a hat? "Well, they could have," I said, and they answered "Good, because if they came from a hat then you can keep them." We all smiled and I was not so grumpy anymore. They stayed quite awhile and chatted about sailing and boats. It was more like a visit from old friends than a customs check. This was just the beginning of the friendliness we would encounter from the people of New Zealand. When we left the customs dock and pulled into the marina, (first marina *Poet's Place* has been to in over three years) our cruising friends met us on the dock with a sack of fresh produce, fresh bread and coins for hot showers at the marina, along with an invite to dinner at the Cruising Club. The cruising community is like family out here.

The Bay of Islands reminds me so much of the San Juan Islands of Washington that at times I felt like I was transformed back. In fact, the entire North Island reminds me of Washington State except for the date palms and the giant fern trees. Everything grows in New

Zealand. Apple trees grow next to orange trees (never seen anything like it), strawberries, raspberries, blueberries, avocados, even bananas, all grow in the same area. My vegetarian soul was in heaven.

Every evening during the passage to New Zealand, part of our entertainment was the *Cruisers radio net*. Of course I was always an active participant on this net. Most boats reported their position, some information about the conditions and then ended with "All is well aboard." Being the honest person that I am, I always described our condition aboard as "shitty" and my condition was "stressful" and I didn't know where the hell the rest of them were, but all was *not* well aboard *Poet's Place*. Upon arriving in Opua and visiting the Opua Cruising Club for dinner our first night, a couple from Austria greeted us with their little five-year-old daughter Anna. They excitedly asked if I was Sharon from *Poet's Place*, as Anna wanted to meet me. They said she listened to my radio net every night and when they arrived in Opua the officials asked Anna how her passage to New Zealand was. Anna replied, "My trip was like Sharon's on Poet's Place, shitty and stressful." Steve said that I was influencing young international children with bad language. I felt like a celebrity for a while.

The tiny and charming waterfront town of Opua has such ambiance. It consists of a small well stocked grocery store, hanging over the water, with a bakery on one side and an ice cream parlor on the other. All the cruisers gained weight while in New Zealand. Then there is the ferry boat which takes people and a few cars back and forth to Russell, my favorite town in New Zealand. Opua has a very friendly and tiny post office where everyone knows everyone, and a funky and lively Opua Cruising Club, where they serve dinners four nights a week for a very reasonable price. The other three nights are open for potlucks and anything else cruisers can think of.

During the day, the clubhouse is open and offers free coffee or tea and is the local hangout of cruisers for anything from ironing your clothes to craft classes, home schooling and chat sessions. Next door is the Opua Marina, a first class marina with hot showers and a lovely laundry room, complete with washtubs with hot and cold water and six washers and dryers along with a nice book exchange. Whether your boat is in the marina or anchored out, as we were, you are welcome to use the marina facilities and the Cruising Club. With so many boats from all over the world staying for the cyclone season, we became a little neighborhood of cruisers in Opua. Several of the ladies started a walking group and did a nine kilometer bush walk along the water about five days a week, exercising our mouths as well as our legs! New Zealand has some beautiful scenic trails and I was always picking a bouquet of wild flowers along the way. We even had our own radio net on VHF at 8:00 a.m. Monday-Friday. It was called the Bay of Islands Cruisers Information Net; each day of the week we had a net controller (radio show host). On Thursday mornings it was *Sharon's Radio Show*. It really kept us all informed. We had a local weatherman. Rides were offered to those without cars. Information was shared about potlucks, concerts, lost and found, etc. Items for sale or trade were offered and that's how we bought our new water maker for two hundred dollars. I never knew my neighbors this well back home.

In most other countries, the price you see is the price you pay. In New Zealand there is either no tax or the tax is included, and tipping is an insult. I could really get used to this.

One of my favorite places in New Zealand is the charming, sleepy little storybook village of Russell. To get there, one must take a ten minute little ferryboat ride from Opua. Russell consists of lovely Victorian homes and English style cottages with white picket fences and flower gardens everywhere. It looks like something out of a fairytale. Everyone in Russell has a view of the water, as the town is situated on the water surrounded by lush rolling green hills. The waterfront is lined with cafes and pubs, markets, stores and lovely cottages, all overlooking the beautiful beach and clear water. The oldest church and graveyard in New Zealand is in the town of Russell. A drive or hike up Flagstaff Hill will reward you with panoramic views of the Bay of Islands with its beautiful blue water dotted with emerald islands. It is quite a sight to behold. When our friends, Pat and Barry, came to visit *Poet's Place* again, we spent a day enjoying the sights of Russell. I think there are more flowers, bluer water and more sunshine in Russell than anywhere else in New Zealand. If I had to live in New Zealand, I would want to live in Russell. I also found a wonderful 12-step AA meeting every Friday night in Russell. A group of us cruisers and Opua locals take the ferry over on Fridays, sometimes enjoying a meal at the waterfront fish and chips place first. I have made some lifetime friends in Russell. The people are as charming as the town.

Like any neighborhood, the cruising community has its share of characters. We have a Canadian, *eh*, named Clifford and I have a love-hate relationship with him. The cruisers decided to have a holiday potluck and wanted me to organize it. I thought it might be nice to let someone else have a chance at doing some of the planning—some new blood, you know. So this bloody bloke (New Zealand talk) of a character named Clifford volunteered. Clifford likes things his way, so he decided we would all eat turkey (not a good choice of meat in New Zealand) and everyone would chip in to pay for the turkey, including vegetarians. Well turkeys in New Zealand aren't cheap, so this potluck was turning into an expensive dinner. Anyone wanting to make stuffing or potatoes or gravy had to use Cliff's recipe. When Annie from Texas found out she couldn't use her cornbread stuffing recipe, she told old Clifford to "Go stuff it!" On the morning of the potluck (Clifford's dinner) old Cliff went to the Cruising Club kitchen to roast his turkeys his way in large plastic bags. He was not pleased to find the ovens at the clubhouse only heated to 300 degrees. He turned the ovens all the way up to 300, put the bagged turkeys in and went back to his boat to relax. When Clifford went back to check on the birds, several hours later, he had a blast of excitement as the bags exploded all over the kitchen and Cliff. Seems old Clifford didn't realize that New Zealand uses Centigrade not Fahrenheit, so the turkeys were roasting at over 650 degrees. I was in charge of all the potlucks after that. The turkeys didn't taste too bad I was told.

I didn't think we could afford to buy a car in New Zealand, but it turned out we couldn't afford not to. The bus system is not as good as it was in Central America. We bought a 1991 Mitsubishi diesel in mint condition for $400US. It had air conditioning, we added new tires and I named her *Miss Bitchy* for Mitsubishi. In the cruising community, half the cruisers bought cars and the other half borrowed the cars from the cruisers who bought them. So we seldom put petrol (gas) in the tank, as the borrowers filled it up each time they borrowed the car. Oh yes, the car came with a steering wheel on the right side. Driving on the left side of the road here takes a little getting used to at first. New Zealand consists of very curvy two-lane roads and one-lane bridges. There are no motorways (freeways) except in Auckland and New Zealanders are known as being the worst drivers in the world (a record they are very proud of). So land cruising is as much of a challenge in New Zealand as ocean cruising.

As long as we had a car, we decided to do a little land cruising and tour the North Island. We went to visit the couple from New Zealand that we met in Rarotonga while Steve was taking his motorcycle-driving test on the left side of the road. He only passed because he followed Brownie. They invited us to visit them when we sailed to New Zealand, a place I said I would never go. We decided to drive to their home to spend Christmas with them. They live about four -hundred miles south of Auckland, so we had a lovely trip touring most of the North Island. Brownie and Celia have a home on several acres with sheep, cattle, a horse, two cats and a dog named Lucy. Since they have a catering business, we had a wonderful Christmas dinner with all the trimmings and many friends of theirs came to join us. After spending several days at Brownie's home, we traveled to the coast not too far away, to visit with old cruising friends from the sailing vessel, *Loafer*. This couple and their three young children, now almost teenagers, sailed with us three years before in California and Mexico before heading out to the South Pacific and then New Zealand. They fell in love with New Zealand

and decided to settle there, buying a home, working and enjoying the kiwi life. It was so nice to see them again and catch up on all the news. We stayed a few days enjoying old friends and then continued on to explore more of the North Island. It was nice to be off the boat, do some land cruising and just play tourist for a while.

Most of the ladies didn't bother to learn left sided driving and were content letting their husbands drive. Not so with me. I knew that if I didn't learn, then I would always be dependent on Steve; heaven knows I needed my independence after living together twenty-four hours a day, seven days a week. So, every Friday five of us ladies piled into *Miss Bitchy* for our ladies day out. As we headed for Kerikeri , the nearest big town, *Miss Bitchy* would stop at every roadside stand, yard sale and interesting place we could find. The chocolate factory was one of our favorites as they gave great samples. Sometimes we'd make it to Kerikeri and sometimes we never did. We just had fun and always stopped for lunch. When we got back from our day of shopping, the back of the car actually dragged on the road from the weight of all our shopping bags. It's amazing how many bags one could stuff into the trunk of *Miss Bitchy.*

Well, on one of these outings, we were talking quite a lot (surprise) and I had forgotten which country I was driving in. I did a little weaving as I turned around to talk with my passengers while driving on the wrong side of the road. Within a few minutes we were pulled over by a young New Zealand police officer. Upon peering into *Miss Bitchy* and viewing five lips sealed and smiling middle-aged ladies, it was all he could do to keep from laughing. He said, "You're either very drunk or a very bad driver." I informed him I was a very bad driver and was still getting used to driving on the opposite side of the road. He said he thought I should practice more with my husband (male chauvinist). They are very backwards here. I never lived this one down, especially with Steve.

Our cruising friends, Phil and Jill, from England, on the sailboat *Deliverance*, also purchased a car while in New Zealand. One morning, on the cruisers net, they announced that their car was missing from the marina car park (parking lot). They had been gone sailing the islands for a few days and upon returning noticed the car was gone. Had anyone seen it? Phil thought he had left the key hanging out of the boot (trunk) and Jill was ready to drown him. Steve thought he had seen the car in town the day before, but knowing Phil and Jill were gone sailing, thought he must be mistaken. That afternoon, we were walking by the car park when we spotted Phil and Jill and the missing car, which had now reappeared. Looking bewildered, Phil explained that the car just reappeared by afternoon and looked very tidy, was all locked up and appeared to be filled with petrol (fuel). Within minutes, the marina manager came running out with another cruising couple (German cruising friends). Seems a poor German back-packer was in need of fifty dollars to take a bus out of town and upon walking through the Opua Marina car park, spotted a key hanging from the boot of one of the cars. His enterprising mind took over and he entered the Opua Cruising Club, finding fellow Germans and asked if they had a car. When they replied no, he asked if they might want to rent one for fifty dollars for two days. What a deal! The German cruising couple quickly said yes. Our young entrepreneur suggested they return the car clean and filled with petrol and return the key to the marina office. In the end, everyone was happy. The young back-packer got his ticket out of town (probably a good thing), our German cruising friends had a two day car rental at a very good rate and Phil and Jill got their car back, clean and filled with petrol. The next day some of us cruisers made a large sign and hung it on both sides of Phil and Jill's car. It read *Deliverance Car Rental call 1-800-STOLEN—Get 'em while there HOT*. Jill now carries the keys to the car.

Steve

The most prestigious race in world sailing is the America's Cup Race. Not a real big deal in America, but it is huge in New Zealand where sailing is their number one national sport. Racing sailors are national sports heroes and when racing is on TV the local sports bars fill up with enthusiastic fans to cheer on the home team.

This year the New Zealand team was defending the title for the coveted America's Cup. And we had a good crowd of sailors from all over the world packing the Opua Yacht Club every race day to watch the event on a big screen TV. We could go over to Auckland and see the event in person but the view is really better on TV. And it is more exciting when you are watching with a good crowd of Kiwi's in a sports bar type atmosphere. Unfortunately Team New Zealand did not fair so well this year; they lost the cup by losing five straight match races against *Alingie* a Swiss sponsored boat from a country that does not even have a seaport. The New Zealanders were very embarrassed and upset being beaten by Switzerland who was just entering the America's Cup for the first time. Of course, half of the Swiss team was from New Zealand. During the race these men had death threats on their life and were labeled traitors by the local media.

The America's Cup was a major economic boom for New Zealand and will be greatly missed, as the next race will be in Europe. It generated about $750 million dollars for New Zealand; this is a huge sum for a small country of four million people. It is unlikely they will be able to finance another winning team, as the cost to compete successfully in the Cup is about $250 million.

It was very exciting as a sailor to be involved in this community where there is so much enthusiasm for sailing. We watched the race with Kiwi friends, Swiss friends and many others from different countries, so there was lots of cheering for both sides. We were very happy for the Swiss but very sad for New Zealand, as this was a very big loss to them.

Sharon
Shortly after being put in charge of the potluck dinners, I decided to add a movie to the agenda, making it the pot-luck/movie night. The Opua Cruising Clubhouse has a TV/VCR, so we just rented videos making this event a very popular one with young and old alike. About a week or two before we flew home, we had our last pot-luck/movie night. Everyone was getting ready to move on.

Some cruisers were flying home for the season, like us, while others were sailing to Fiji or Tonga, Hawaii or back to Canada or the States. Many of us had been cruising together off and on for two to four years and all of us had been together for the past five months of cyclone season. It was like saying goodbye to family. The whole neighborhood was moving. We all cried, even big burley guys were crying like babies. I read one of my poems about goodbye and the place was flooded. Then the cruisers read a poem they had written for me. I couldn't see through my tears. Just thinking about it makes my eyes water. Here is the poem they wrote. It seems to describe me pretty well. Enjoy!

"Sharon"

Sharon is her name
From Seattle she and Steve came
Poet's Place got them across the Pacific
Even though the trip was anything but terrific
When the winds didn't blow and the engine didn't go
The passage was uncomfortable and slow
Potlucks and movies she prepared
No butter or meat, please, she declared.
She is well known as a good walker.
But no one can surpass her as a talker.
Thursdays she did her morning road show
Friday evenings to her meetings she did go.
The girls she would take shopping,
But not without a lot of stopping
For anything that was free
That's where Sharon would be
"You're a really bad driver," said the cop.
But her humor never did stop
She may seem like a princess from a story,
When Steve is rowing her in the dory.
But known as a grandmother too
She proudly sports a gecko tattoo
She has been known to cut hair for hours
As well as picking many flowers

162

She openly bemoans the cold.
But she is a wonderful Poet to behold
Her relationship with Cliff may be strained
But her friendship we have all gained
For six months she will be away
For a little work and lots of play
The quiet airways we will enjoy
Until her return to us - Oh Boy!

Home

Sharon Reed-Hendricks

Home is not a building
Home is not a town
Home's a place within your heart
And you carry it around

Home's a combination
Of the places you have been
The people and the memories
That your heart carries within

Home is always with you
It is not left far behind
It's the heart and soul within you
And the peacefulness you find

Home is where you'll always be
Even when you're far away
You are home - It's in your heart
And home is where you'll stay

13 The Visit Back Home

Sharon

It's hard to believe we've been home to Seattle and now we're back home in New Zealand. I'm not sure where home is any more, except that home is *Poet's Place;* wherever she is must be home for us. It's also difficult to believe that it is springtime again and summer is soon to arrive. Everything is blooming, birds are singing and the weather is warming. When we arrived in Seattle in May, it was springtime. It soon turned to one of the best summers that Seattle has ever seen. We stayed to feel the chill in the air and see the leaves start to turn and we knew it was time to head south and repeat the cycle. We just skipped winter altogether. I think that's the way life should be lived, just skip over winter. I missed *Poet's Place* so much and it is good to be back, but I also miss the grandchildren, the kids and friends we left back home. It is difficult being a gypsy. I wish I could just bring everyone with me to share the adventure, but since I can't, then this book will have to do.

There is a price to pay for everything in life, and I pay the high price of missing all my friends and family to be out here cruising. We left Seattle the 23rd of September and arrived in Auckland the 25th of September, skipping Wednesday the 24th altogether as we crossed the date line. It was another long flight with plane changes in Canada and Hawaii and flying all night from Hawaii to Auckland. Upon finding our seats on Air New Zealand out of Hawaii, we looked behind us a few rows and there were our longtime cruising friends, Tony and Linda Keeling flying back to their boat in New Zealand also. They have a condo in Hawaii and had been home for the summer too. What a small world. I changed seats with Tony for a while so I could catch up with Linda after all these months and it made the flight time go faster.

After clearing customs at the airport, we were picked up by the hostel (more like a Bed and Breakfast) van and taken to our lovely

room. I had made reservations via the internet to stay overnight in Auckland to catch up on some much needed rest after
traveling some thirty hours. It's an additional four-hour drive to
Opua, where *Poet's Place* is moored, and I couldn't fathom
any more traveling until I got some sleep. Steve, on the other hand,
thought nothing of continuing on, but I quickly vetoed that. And
I'm very glad I did. I also took echinacea one week before and one
week after the flight to build my immune system (don't laugh, it
works). Guess who got sick two days after arriving back. Steve's
not laughing anymore and I've been feeling great. In New Zealand they have wonderful hostels that I would recommend to anyone traveling around New Zealand. They are much less expensive
than hotels and just as nice, if not nicer. We had our own room
and bath and since it's in a home-like setting, you get use of the
kitchen and the laundry. That way you can do your own cooking
and your laundry. You also get to meet a number of other travelers
from all over the world.

For fifty-three dollars we stayed at a lovely hostel. Most are even
less expensive, so it's sure the way to travel around the country. I
don't know why the States doesn't adopt this system. We found out
that the bus into downtown Auckland ran directly in front of our
hostel. So after a little nap, we hopped on a bus into downtown and
played tourist for the day. It was a lovely warm spring day and we
took a ferry over to a little township across the bay. It seemed so
strange that just a few weeks previously we had taken a ferry from
downtown Seattle to Bainbridge Island. The two cities of Auckland
and Seattle are so similar, no wonder it felt so much like home. We
had a great day and a good night's sleep and were ready the next
morning for our cruising friends, Will and Annie, who were car
sitting our car, to come pick us up. We spent the next night at their
home as they were renting a place for the winter so they could
work on their boat and not live aboard. This enabled us to get two
good nights of sleep before returning to *Poet's Place* after almost
five months of being left on a mooring.

Annie and Will had taken good care of the car. We decided

Miss Bitchy was in need of a bath. After cleaning her inside and out we made the drive to Opua. On the drive through the windy country roads, I realized that I was seeing New Zealand northland through new eyes. I guess leaving and coming back gave me a new prospective on things. The rolling green hills looked even greener and more lush than I had remembered and the flowers more colorful and beautiful. Sheep and dairy cows dotted the hillsides. Palm trees and ferns, orange groves and grape vineyards, kiwi and berries filled in the scenery. I realized then how privileged I am to be not just a visitor, but also a temporary resident of these beautiful countries that I sail to. *Poet's Place* is the sailing home that enables me to be "home" wherever I am.

Paihia (nine kilometers from Opua) and Opua are seaside towns with beautiful beaches and water of various shades of blue. The shops in Paihia are situated along the water, much like a California coastal town, with the beach and surf across the street. Opua reminds me much of Friday Harbor, Washington, without the big town. It felt familiar and comforting.

When we arrived in Opua our Kiwi friends, Pam and Dene, met us on the dock to ferry us out to our mooring where *Poet's Place* had been waiting for our return. She looked good but also very lonely and deserted. I was worried she would be covered with green mold from the wet winter but she only had a little around the edges. When we opened her up I expected her to smell musty, but instead, she smelled good and on the table was a fresh baked loaf of bread and some veggies. Pam and Dean had done a great job of looking after *Poet's Place*. Pam had even laundered my towels. There is nothing that compares to the cruising community. Over and over, I am reminded of what a fantastic group of friends we are privileged to have in this close knit community of cruisers. The same holds true of our circle of friends back home who are always there for us. We feel so blessed.

It took us a week to unpack the four huge duffel bags and two big backpacks we brought back from the States. One bag at a time was

167

all the boat or I could handle. In fact I'm not sure how we made it on the airline without paying extra for being overweight. One of the bags weighed over seventy-five pounds. It was so big it took two guys to handle it and one little lady two days to unpack it. In order to make room for all the stuff we brought back with us, I had to do a spring-cleaning and toss out many items. I found some mold and mildew hiding in many places, so I took apart, washed and cleaned every inch of *Poet's Place*. It took about ten days and I found things I had forgotten we had. Seems funny to size down when we've already sized down to a thirty-seven foot sailboat, yet I felt like I had way too many things. Some items we put aside to sell at the boater's swap meet next month and some things we gave away or just tossed. After being back in the consumer U.S. for five months, I realized that most people have way too much stuff. Nobody needs all that stuff. In all of the countries I have visited so far, the people have so much less yet they are so much happier. We need so little, yet we have so much and we want more. The world is teaching me a valuable lesson and I am slowly learning that less is really more. With all that said, there is one thing you can't have too much of, and that is friends and loved ones. And I just love all my friends. It was so wonderful to see and spend time with so many friends, family and grandchildren.

After three years of being away, it seemed so strange to be back in the States. In some ways it was as if we'd been gone forever, and yet sometimes it seemed like we had never been away. Much has changed, grown and disappeared. More rules than I remember. More people, more traffic, more paranoia, just more everything. Yes, a lot has changed, especially me. I have changed. My outlook has changed. This new perspective emerged on our voyage and I continue to grow. I now look at the U.S. through the eyes of the world. It is still my home, but it is not the best nor the greatest anymore. This may sound un-patriotic but I have seen the damage the U.S. government has done abroad. I think we have been brainwashed in this country. I still love so many things about the States but my views on our government have changed.

168

Steve

What a great summer we had visiting everyone and I was so glad we could spend five months. T.S. Eliot said it this way, "We shall not cease from exploration and the end of all our exploring will be to arrive where we started and know the place for the first time." When we first got back to Seattle we thought things sure had changed. But slowly we realized things had not changed that much, but our perspective had changed dramatically. After living in two-dozen other countries we have learned the American Way is not the only way. We have learned most people in these counties have more personal freedom than we do in the U.S. We learned people in most countries do not have as much stuff as Americans, but they do not have to work as hard and have a lot more time for family and friends. They are happy with what they have. We have learned that 99 per cent of people everywhere want to be friends and they want to be helpful. We have learned that the less people have, the more friendly they tend to be. The more people have, the more they tend to be afraid and lock themselves away from others. Americans seem to be the most afraid, with security check points everywhere, gated communities, security systems, and extra deadbolts on every door, not to mention a loaded gun in the closet, plus six insurance policies to cover every possible threat or calamity. And now we have a *Department of Homeland Security* to heighten the paranoia even more with yellow, orange and red alerts announced daily like weather bulletins. What is our country coming to and what are we afraid of.

We feel safe and secure in the cruising life. We have lots of very good friends who have time for us and who we can count on when we need them. We know that wherever we go, we will make more good friends and hopefully we will spread a little love and goodwill for America. Will we ever move back to the States? We really don't know. Nowhere is there freedom like on the open ocean where we are responsible for our own destiny and free to sail wherever the wind will take us.

It was good to come home to get a better perspective on our cruising life. And it is good to live in other countries to get a new outlook and to know our own country for the first time. I think if we live in any one place for too long we begin to lose perspective on the world, so we may just keep moving on.

Sharon
One of the best reasons for coming home was to see and spend time with the grandchildren. When we left for this adventure four years ago, we had two grandchildren and now we have eight. So you see, we needed to re-acquaint ourselves with the older ones and meet some of the new ones.

We had some great get-togethers, barbeques and dinners with our kids. Staying in their homes for sometimes weeks at a time, you really get to know their families, sometimes more than you want. At times, I'm just as glad I don't live too close as it may be too tempting to interfere. And there are times I feel I am missing some of their growing-up years and maybe I'm not there enough for them. Yet, when we come to visit with all our stories and pictures, there is a closeness that develops and maybe they will know that they too can someday live their dream. I think our oldest grandson Cody summed it up when we came to his school to do a slide presentation of our adventures. He said, "All the kids in my class wish they had grandparents like mine, cause all their grandparents do is sit around and mine do exciting things."

All the kids seemed to enjoy the seashells and homemade gifts from far away more than store bought ones. Each gift came with a story behind it. Once again I am reminded that *less is really more,* including time spent with grandchildren. It's quality not quantity. Across every ocean and every country I visit, I take all eight of these grandchildren with me in my heart.

It was a busy time for us, visiting with family and friends and giving about thirty slide show presentations for sailing clubs, schools, organizations and in private homes. In addition, both Steve and I worked jobs for the summer season. I worked my old summer job on Jetty Island for the city of Everett Parks Department. Steve worked for West Marine, the marine hardware store. We needed the money and this experience, to know we really don't want to be back in the *rat race*. It was good for us to come back, not just for a visit, but to live and work again in this world. It helped me to realize that I really do love the cruising life and I'm not ready to come back.

We did a bit of house sitting, until our friend Nam offered his small sailboat at our old marina in Everett on the very same dock where we use to live on *Poet's Place*. It was almost like going back four years. I bought a bike and biked to the Jetty ferry dock and Steve walked about one mile to work. It actually worked out great as most things in life do. Our future son-in-law, Leon loaned us one of his vehicles so we had wheels to go visiting on our days off.

It was a wonderful summer. The weather in Seattle was warm and I loved every minute of it. Work was fun, but I am not use to working a forty plus hour week and found I was exhausted by end of day. We also found that the cost of living in Seattle area is so high that just food and fuel took much of our money. We were lucky we didn't have rent to pay or a car payment and other things like insurance that would have cleaned us out. We could never afford to live in Seattle again. It's so much cheaper and easier to live out there sailing.

Haul-Out Hotel
When we arrived back in New Zealand it was time once again for much needed maintenance. Every couple of years, a boat needs a bottom job, which means hauling her out of the water. You then need to scrub, sand and fill, then paint the bottom (keel and rudder). If you are not handy, or if you are very rich, you can hire someone to do this for you. We are handy and poor. *Poet's Place* had not had a bottom job in three years so we were long over-due. Since we were out of the water anyway, we decided it was time to sand and paint the hull and topsides also. This is a job we did eight

171

years ago and I swore I would never do again. We also re-painted the dinghy. So as you can see, were very busy for over two months.

Being on the hard, in *haul-out hotel* as I call it, is not fun. You have no toilet to flush (need salt water for that), our refrigerator is water cooled so we have no refrigerator and to get to land one must descend a twelve-foot ladder. The good part (there is always a good part) is that we are not alone—we have heaps of company. Three of our English cruising friends are hauled out along with our Kiwi friends Pam and Dene and several other cruisers (about 15 of us) so it's like a little neighborhood. I've also been working a few hours a week down at the little Opua store, which is situated hanging over the water next to the ferry dock and only a short walk from the marine/boat yard. It's actually kind of fun. I only work a few mornings a week from 7:00 a.m. to 9:00 a.m. making deli sandwiches. I get to know the local folks and get some nice perks like free sandwiches and bread from the bakery. Since they can't pay me cash, because I'm not a kiwi, we trade for food. This works out great for me and gets me going early a few mornings a week. The weather has not warmed up enough for me yet at 60 to 75 degrees, but then it never does. I am determined to enjoy my time left in New Zealand, maybe cruising the bay of islands more and some land travel to the South, as I may never be back this way again. But then we never know, do we, when we'll be back again. I was thinking the other day, that when I'm very, very old (about 102) and I die and go wherever that place is, I think the place would have twenty-four hour sunshine and all the friends I have ever known in my lifetime. Then I could spend all my time just visiting and talking with everyone. We would have such fun because we would all have time to spend with each other—an eternity. That, for me, would be heaven.

A Different Way

Sharon Reed-Hendricks

We rush and stress most everyday
For things we need and bills to pay
Alarms and clocks - we won't be late
In lines and traffic jams we wait

Phones that ring and beepers blare
And then we breathe polluted air
Grab fast food and watch TV
No! This is not the life for me

And so I choose a different way
A slower pace for everyday
A life without TV or phones
Without a car - no bills no loans

Without these things I feel so free
With less I have more - time for me
More time to just set sail and go
Whichever way the wind will blow

14 Haul Out in New Zealand

Sharon

Seventy-three days! That's how long we were on the hard. They call it the hard because it's not easy. A boat belongs in the water, not twenty feet in the air in a noisy, dusty boatyard with a twelve-foot ladder attached to its side and a garland of paint cans, sandpaper, rags and assorted tools surrounding the keel. As if that weren't enough, your toilet doesn't work, your refrigerator doesn't cool and your sink drain empties on the tools at the bottom of the boat. Life is hard on the hard but it's part of cruising. They tell you how many days when you go to pay the bill, seventy-three days. Actually it was seventy-four, but who's counting as the first day is free. The first six weeks we spent sanding and grinding, then more sanding and grinding until I thought we would sand a hole right through the hull. Then we put on two coats of primer, three coats of undercoat and three coats of two-part polyurethane paint with sanding in-between each coat.

For about seven weeks she looked like a derelict and I was wondering if we should have ever started this project in the first place. We did it ourselves by the roll and tip method. They said we couldn't do it and that it had to be sprayed on by professionals. But we had done it before by ourselves and knew we could do it again. Yet I worried and wondered, as it had been eight years and it was a lot of work then. Could we really do this job ourselves? Was it really worth all the work we were putting ourselves through? I was even beginning to think we would live in Ashby's boatyard in Opua forever, so I started to plant a garden. While Steve filled and sanded for the umpteenth time, I re-varnished all the teak wood on the boat and the dinghy. I'm not sure who looked dustier by the end of the day— the boat or us. In hindsight (isn't hindsight wonderful) it was worth it! The new paint job we gave her makes her look like new, in fact I think she looks even better than she did eight years ago when we did this. The guys from the professional paint shed were impressed. We had so many people stop by to admire our paint job that our heads were swelling. Even the representative from the paint company said he had never seen one done by hand that looked so good.

It was every bit as much work as it was the first time, maybe more, as we are eight years older. The most significant change is the blue dolphins painted along the haul where a blue stripe used to be. It was my idea really, as I wanted something different. Everyone has a white boat with a stripe or stripes of various *colour* (New Zealand spelling). Or, they have a dark boat with a white stripe. Our friend, Dene on S/V *Wayfarer*, a local kiwi artist/cruiser had volunteered to paint our name, *Poet's Place* on our newly painted topsides. What he didn't know was my great idea of the dolphins. Steve thought I was crazy. Dene didn't know what he had got himself into when we sat down to discuss script for a name and ended up sketching dolphins, forty-eight on each side, swimming along our topsides. It took Dene three full days to hand paint two coats of blue dolphins for a total of one-hundred-ninety-two dolphins. It is so unique and gives the boat a totally new look. Then Steve worked three days on Dene's boat fixing his radio and refrigerator. We love the barter system. We had also sanded and painted our three-part nested dinghy while in the yard. We used the same system and paint on the outside of the dinghy and I painted the inside too. Well that's a story in itself.

Steve told me to go pick out any colour paint I wanted for the inside of the dinghy (also called a dink). So my friend Diane, who was also living in the boat yard, went along with me to pick out paint. In the past we had always had a beige colour inside, as white is too bright. We picked out what we thought was close to the old beige, they called it Sand Storm. As they mixed it, I thought the Sand Storm looked a little rosy. But dusty rose is nice. As I painted the inside of the dink I thought the bright sunshine made it look a little brighter pink than I remembered in the store. By the time I was finished and the sun was setting, everyone in the boatyard was commenting on the glow of bright pink from the inside of our dink. Steve wanted to know why I choose bright pink. I told him it wasn't pink, it was beige. He asked everyone in the yard, even children, what colour it was. They would open and shut their eyes as if they were stinging and reply "Pink!" And so a decision was made to change the colour ASAP. Steve thought if he mixed some white with the left over pink we would have a more subtle shade. It turned dark gray and I refused to apply it. Another trip to the store, this time to mix so many samples that I thought the clerk was going to throw me out. As I started to apply the new paint we noticed it looked white as I went too far the other way. Then we added some of Steve's gray paint. By this time I really didn't care what colour it was, I just wanted it done. Over the bright pink, the new colour turned out light lilac, almost beige when the sun shines on it.

And so on the 18th of December, one week before Christmas, *Poet's Place* pulled up roots (they really were growing), was launched, and floated again. The night before we had a launching party with about fifty other cruising friends, complete with potluck and a beautiful sunset. Dene is now in demand for dolphin painting.

In Opua we have a local resident doctor who lives on his boat at the marina. His wife is the administrator at the Bay of Islands hospital and Dr. Geoff has a practice nearby. Dr. Geoff and Raewin have sold their home and are getting ready to go cruising next year. They have become great mates (friends) of ours. Dr. Geoff has made himself available to cruisers from 7:00 a.m. to 6:00 p.m.; it is great having a doctor in the neighborhood. I had a couple of moles that needed to be removed, one of them just needed to be frozen off, so Dr. Geoff just made a boat call while we were in the boatyard and zapped my mole with his freeze gun. A few weeks later he did surgery on another mole in his office after hours. Steve worked on Geoff's boat doing rigging for a couple of days. I could get use to this barter system very easily.

It seemed strange having Christmas in summer. The ads for Christmas in New Zealand center on barbeques and picnics at the beach. It stays light outside till 9:30 p.m. at night so it really doesn't feel like Christmas. Mind you, I love it. Since most cruisers are away from family for the holidays and we don't like being lonely, we all got together for a big Christmas day potluck at the Opua cruising club. That year there were seventy-seven of us and what a feast it was. We had twelve countries represented. I was in charge of games and entertainment (surprise!). We had a get-acquainted game where people had to find someone from Norway or someone over seventy years old, and so on. It got everyone to mingle. We also had a white elephant gift exchange that was a hoot. I was in my glory as the Master's of Ceremony of entertainment.

Possum's Place
A few weeks after we were back on anchor, I got up early one morning to get ready for work and looked outside in the cockpit. I noticed that my mesh bag of oranges that I always keep outside, looked as though a bomb had exploded in it. All over the cockpit were bits of oranges; orange rinds, pulp and juice were plastered everywhere. I called Steve to look at the bombsight and asked him what he thought had happened. He said, it must be the birds but that was strange, as sea gulls don't usually eat fruit. I couldn't believe that, because for four years I had always kept oranges and bananas in the cockpit, even when anchored off bird sanctuary islands and never once did any birds even pick at an orange. After breakfast we went outside and Steve got the dinghy ready as I started to pick up the mess in the cockpit. I noticed there were heaps of little print marks all over the deck and thought: *boy there must have been a whole flock of birds*. Then I noticed some items spilled out of a little cubbyhole and when I went to put an item back I screamed as I saw this furry thing lying there. "Steve, there's a rat in our cockpit," I screamed. Steve informed me it was a possum and proceeded to get the camera and take several photos while I screamed to get the bloody thing off the boat now! Steve said I would be late for work so he would row me in and come back later to get the possum (over my dead body). I didn't care how late I was, he was going to get that thing off the boat now! I asked him not to kill it, but to get it with the fish net and toss it overboard. As Steve was starting to net him, Mr. Possum ran, took a high dive and leaped overboard. He started to swim over to the next boat and half way over the ugly critter stopped, turned around

and looked at me as if to say, "I'll be back." Possums swim very well.

Our *possum story* was announced over the local radio net and now everyone is calling us *Possum's Place*. If you remember, we've had snakes on board in Mexico and Panama, and now a possum in New Zealand. Thanks to our low freeboard it seems to be easy for critters to board our yacht. I'm not sure I want to go to Australia as we'll probably have crocodiles in the cockpit.

While in New Zealand, one of the men in my AA group from Russell had invited Steve and I to visit his farm. We thought this would be interesting as Steve use to live on a farm and it would be nice to see what a small New Zealand farm was like. We were hoping to see a few sheep and maybe some cattle and a nice little garden. As we drove down the long driveway of this farm, the iron gates opened with a view of the tennis courts and then farther back the swimming pool. There on the ridge overlooking a small lake and acres and acres (twenty-two-thousand acres) of rolling green pastures, sat the sprawling, modern ranch house. I turned to Steve and said, "I don't think this is a small farm experience." Ian and Ann came out to welcome us to their farm and insisted that we have lunch with them out by the pool. After lunch it took all afternoon and into the evening for Ian to drive us around his farm and show us his seven-thousand sheep and five-thousand head of cattle, along with assorted other animals and the farm manager's home, assistant manager's home, the shepherd's home, the lake, assorted barns and other buildings. The most interesting building is the sheep-shearing barn where they shear four sheep at a time. We asked if we could come and visit sometime when they shear the sheep and Ann said she would let us know and we were certainly welcome to come. We now know a ranch the size of Bonanza is known in New Zealand as a *farm*. We found out Ann, Ian's wife, has a farm of her own in the south part of the North Island and it's much larger than Ian's farm. I'm not sure we will have the time to tour her farm.

Steve
Ian's wife, Ann called us to let us know they were shearing sheep

179

and invited us to join them on the farm. The sheep here are sheared twice a year. A professional team of sheep shearers comes in to do the job as quick and efficiently as possible. This was a two-day job for a crew of ten people, four men shearing thirty-five-hundred ewes and six helpers packing wool and sorting sheep with the help of two keen sheep dogs. These guys were fascinating to watch. They can sheer a sheep in two minutes or less, but it is hard backbreaking work. They got paid $2NZ per sheep, but they have to split that with the rest of their crew. It is good money for New Zealand but a hard life moving every few days to a new farm. And if it rains, as it often does, they have to wait for the sheep to dry out. The day we were watching it started to rain, so they had the dogs herd about five-hundred ewes into holding pens under the shearing barn to keep them dry.

Sheep dog trial clubs are a big sport in New Zealand. There are many clubs of people training purebred dogs for herding competition. But these have little to do with real farm dogs. The real working sheep dogs here might be of any breed. The farm we were visiting had ten dogs, all crossbred mutts, some for working cattle and some for sheep. They really are an important part of the farm and they love their work.

For most of our travels we have felt very safe, welcome and respected by people everywhere. But things are changing. I've been taking an informal poll of what Kiwi's and Europeans here really think about we Americans these days. What they are saying (when I pin them down) is most people they know feel we are rather arrogant, rude and maybe stupid. They cite our actions with Iraq as an example confirming their belief of American arrogant behavior. The locals still smile when we pay our bill and they gladly take our money. However, when we ask for something they don't have, some have rather rudely reminded us we are not in America. Many of us here are sensing a real negative shift in attitudes toward Americans. Hopefully things will improve, but it is a bit worrisome when our president and our foreign policy seem to have a negative influence on what the world thinks of us.

Sharon

One of the reasons we liked basing ourselves in Opua is that it is in the Bay of Islands (much like the San Juan Islands in Washington) and we can up anchor anytime and day sail to one of the islands. So after all the boat work in the yard, we decided to go sailing the islands once we got launched. We took off for a couple of weeks after Christmas, as the weather that summer was marvelous. It was warm and sunny everyday with a light afternoon breeze for sailing.

The first weekend out we sailed over to Russell, my favorite little town in New Zealand, as they were hoisting the Tall Ships Race. Sailing ships from all over New Zealand and the world were there. What a sight! About three-hundred boats entered the race plus a few hundred more just watching. We did not enter, as we are not a tall ship, but had a great time watching from our little boat and taking pictures. After the race and the awards, first prize went to a boat sailed by a couple in their 80's. We then had a traditional Maori hangi.

The Maoris are the native Polynesian New Zealander and their traditional feast is called a hangi. Much like the Hawaiian luau or the Cook Islands umukai, the hangi is cooked in the ground. Once the race was underway, Steve and I went to shore and got to watch the preparation for this feast. We actually knew some of the Maori people preparing the hangi and it was fascinating to watch them in their traditional role and singing in their native language. This was considered one of the largest hangi in New Zealand, as they served one-thousand people. A huge hole was dug in the ground where rocks filled the bottom and banana leaves lined the sides. The rocks held the heat and the banana leaves helped keep it moist. They then placed racks of wrapped meals and seafood carried by four big men with hooks (they were called hookers) and layered them into the ground. I never saw so much food.

There were one-thousand foiled wrapped meals, each one consisted of a large piece of chicken, pork, beef and lamb along with regular and sweet potatoes, a pile of stuffing and a large portion of assorted vegetables. There were racks of clams, oysters and mussels—more seafood than I had ever seen. All this was stacked in the underground oven and covered with more banana leaves and several wet burlap sacks to keep it steaming. It cooked all day. At 7:00 p.m. they uncovered the oven and within less than an hour, served one-thousand people. I never saw anything like it. It was very organized and no waiting. We all sat on the lovely grass overlooking the bay of islands. For $10NZ you got a huge foil-wrapped hangi plus all the seafood you could eat. They had the racks of seafood out on huge tables, allowing you to go back as often as you want and help yourself to clams, oysters and mussels. Steve went back five times. He says only four, but I counted. And he also ate my meat. After the hangi they had a dance. Well actually two dances; one outside with a rock band for the younger group and one inside the Russell Boat Club was the band that played for the older folks where we hung out. It was a wonderful experience and one we will remember fondly.

Leaving Russell, we sailed to some of the little islands in the Bay of Islands. They are lovely with trails and beaches and nice bays to anchor in the protected waters. The water was clear so we went for a swim. Well, Steve went for a swim and I popped in and popped out. New Zealand water is not warm enough for me at 73 degrees. I'm spoiled by the tropics where the water is about 85 degrees. We had a great time exploring the islands before cyclone season was over and we would head to Fiji. We were more than ready to see someplace new, but we will always treasure the memories of our time here and the friends we have made.

The Flow of Friendship

Sharon Reed-Hendricks

Some friends will stay for a long time
And others come and go
They touch our lives when our paths cross
From them we learn and grow

Our friends do not belong to us
They are here by their free choice
We can't control or tie them down
They must speak their own voice

And so my friends flow in and out
Our lives do not stand still
Just like the ocean's ebb and tide
They come by their free will

Sometimes we're going the same place
But we get there different ways
And even when we are apart
Our friendship always stays

So, when our paths go separate ways
I care, though we're apart
'Cause when my friends are not with me
They're carried in my heart

Sometimes we follow different dreams
Until our paths cross once again
You've touched my life - you've touch my heart
You'll always be my friend

15 Passage to Fiji

Sharon

While we were cruising, I wrote a newsletter of our adventures so that friends and family could read about our travels. I also wrote articles for some of the sailing magazines. I would then send these newsletters to my friend Eileen in Seattle, who would edit, print and mail them out. She was a friend and a mentor. On March 15th, 2004, Eileen Geithman passed away after a nineteen month battle with breast cancer. Over the past five years of cruising she has been my cheerleader. She was always encouraging and when I got down she would say, "You have got to keep going, we have a newsletter to get out." She really enjoyed doing the newsletter and toward the end, when I thought it was too much for her, she said it gave her something else to think about instead of chemo. I miss her so much. The newsletter that April was nearly finished and somehow Eileen's husband Glenn managed to complete it and send it out. We can't thank him enough.

On April 28th, after many weeks of waiting for a good weather window, we left New Zealand for Fiji. It was a bittersweet exit. New Zealand will always be my home-away-from-home but the winter weather (as I was bundled up in woolies) was pushing me North to the warmer tropics.

By nightfall, the first day out, we were into heavy seas and 35 knots winds. We were crashing into the wind and seas and for the first time ever in my life, I got seasick. I mean, I got really deathly seasick. For three hours straight I threw up. Then it came out the other end at the same time. First I thought I was going to die and then I wished I would. I started to shake. I was so cold even with long-johns and a heavy jacket. Steve had to hove-to (which means he stopped the boat and we bobbed like a cork) so I could rest. He fixed me a hot water bottle that I hugged and then slept for four hours. After my rest I did feel a little better (there was nothing left to throw up) and we continued on through the horrible seas and wind.

185

On top of all that, we were cold, wet and crabby. The boat was underwater more than on top. We couldn't sit in the cockpit without getting drenched. Water came in via chain plates getting everything in the lockers soaked with saltwater. Then we tore our main headsail, so we had to continue with a storm sail, which is smaller and slowed us down considerably. Even Steve had to agree this was one of our worst passages to date. We weren't alone, as most everyone making the passage that year had a bad one.

I started a radio net for all of the yachts on this passage. I called it the *I-HOP Net* (I Hate Ocean Passages). Everyone agreed by the time a week had passed, they too hated ocean passages. We all got to complain on the radio every morning to each other and I think that helped us feel a little better (misery loves company).

The horrible conditions continued for eleven days when, finally, we reached Minerva Reef. This is a good size circular reef out in the middle of the Pacific Ocean about two thirds of the way to Fiji. You enter through an opening in the reef and can actually anchor in about twenty feet of water. It is really awesome to anchor in the middle of the ocean. The reef, which is shaped like a horse-shoe is only visible above the water at low tide. Otherwise you can see it underwater when the sun is out, as the water is crystal clear and a most beautiful shade of blue. The afternoon we arrived at the reef, the winds were still blowing 30 knots and we had started the engine to help us enter the passage through the reef. Just as we were halfway through the passage, our engine quit. This is very scary when you have reefs on either side of you.

Luckily our friends Paul and Mary were leaving as they had been there four days and needed to head for Tonga. I couldn't believe our luck. We threw them a line and they towed us through the pass. Once inside we continued under sail to the other side of the lagoon inside the reef and dropped anchor in a 25 knots wind and calm seas. Steve fixed the motor at anchor. The next day was Mother's Day and I was one happy mother. If there was any land here I might have stayed forever and became a resident. We stayed four days and enjoyed some wonderful snorkeling on the reef and saw some beautiful fish, reef tipped sharks and coral. I guess Steve is use to the sharks but I continue to get knots in my stomach when they swim too close. I slept ten hours a night. After four days the winds had subsided and we left for the rest of the passage to Fiji.

The passage from Minerva Reef to Fiji took seven more days and it was like someone had turned on a switch for the better. All of a sudden it was warm and sunny, the breezes were gentle and the seas were calmer. We wore bathing suits or nothing at all, so when a wave splashed you it actually felt good. And each sunset was better than the last. Finally, we were in the tropics and I was loving it.

We even caught a beautiful yellow-fin tuna, about forty pounds. I love fresh fish, but this was ridiculous. I suggested we toss it back but Steve would have nothing to do with that idea. We have a small fridge but no freezer, so we were eating fish for every meal and I was getting tired of fish. Then, on the *I-HOP Net*, a cruiser from Australia gave me a recipe for pickled fish. So I actually canned fish while under way.

On May 15th, three days before landfall, I celebrated my fifty-eighth birthday at sea. Several other May birthdays were celebrated at sea so we all decided to have one big celebration when we got to Fiji.

On May 18th at about 10:00 a.m. we made landfall in Savusavu, Fiji. We took a mooring ball at the Copra Shed Marina in SavuSavu Bay. Savusavu is set against a gorgeous backdrop of towering green, mist-shrouded mountains and consists of one main drag about half a km long and faces the water. It looks like a "wild west" town, only in pastels. There is a wonderful open market with very cheap prices. In fact everything in Fiji is inexpensive and the rate of exchange is about

187

two to one. For one of our U.S. dollars we received two Fiji dollars.

Savusavu has several very good restaurants. Our favorite was the Pink Sea View Café where we could eat for $3F each. That's only about $1.50US, and it provided us with more than we could eat.

Steve
What a relief sailing into Savusavu Harbor in the early morning. We took a mooring ball in front of the legendary Copra Shed Marina. The Copra Shed sits on a beautiful, small natural harbor. The bay is small, deep and mirror flat. Hot springs bubble out of the hillside and flow steaming hot water through the village and into the bay causing mystical plumes of steam to rise off the shoreline. After eighteen days of rough sailing in the southern ocean it looked like a mystical Shangri-La. Because the harbor is small, anchoring space is limited so the Copra Shed Marina provides mooring balls to help squeeze in about twenty-five yachts at a time. The Copra Shed houses a good restaurant/bar and several other small businesses in the most idyllic setting imaginable. It's just the kind of place wayward sailors like to get together and hangout for a long time. In fact some of them never leave.

Sharon
I might add there is a reason everything is so lush and green in Savusavu (in fact everywhere this side of the island group). It rained everyday but three, in the three weeks we were there.

Savusavu is a port of entry so a yacht must clear customs here before cruising to other parts of Fiji. The clearing procedure was very easy. Officials came to the boat and couldn't have been nicer. We stayed here three weeks mending our torn sail and doing repairs to the boat from the passage.

188

Upon seeing you for the first time, the people of Fiji don't just approach and ask where you're from. They say something like this: "Hello, you must have just arrived. What day can you come to my village and have dinner?" They love to have you visit their village. In fact, if you are in Fiji long enough you may soon get villaged-out. I might also add about the custom of kava drinking. When invited to visit a village for the first time you are expected to bring a gift of kava. Kava is made from the root of the kava plant, which is dried and then pounded into a fine powder. The kava powder is placed in a silk cloth and soaked in a huge bowl (kava bowl) of water. It looks like mud or dirty dishwater and tastes about the same.

Upon arriving at a village, you must present your packaged kava root (not the powder) to the chief. Kava can be purchased at most open markets already bundled for this purpose. Every village has a chief. It's like going back in time two-hundred years, only instead of eating you for dinner, as was the custom then, they now have you join them for kava drinking. You sit in a circle, crossed legged, men and women must wear a sulu (wrap around cloth) and wait for the coconut cup full of kava to be passed to you. Guests are always first and sometimes, in certain villages, women are not invited unless you are a guest (my luck). When you are handed the cup, you clap once, drink the mud in one big gulp, then hand the cup back and clap three more times. In between, they give speeches in the Fijian language, so this kava drinking can take hours. I have now done so many kava ceremonies that I have become numb to the taste. 0h yes, it numbs your lips, and if you drink enough it makes you sleepy. Hence comes the term "grog" used by locals. The women don't always like the men drinking grog when they should be working. Some things are the same everywhere.

While in Savusavu, between repairs, we had many interesting experiences. We took a bus trip to Labasa, across the mountains to the other side of Vanua Levu. It took three hours, but was a fascinating trip through breathtaking lush mountains. We were also there for the Indian weeklong festival, which was a bit like being in Bombay.

About half of Fiji's population is Indian. Steve even got involved in the Rotary Club and helped a local village.

Steve
I visited the local Savusavu Rotary Club (as a past Rotarian) and they welcomed me with open arms. I went with a few members to help donate a generator to a village in the bush, where they lived by kerosene lamp. I ended up being the honored guest speaker representing "Rotary International." It was a great time. We were treated like royalty with a huge feast and lots of kava ceremony.

Sharon
If you look at a map of Fiji you will see that it consists of two main islands. Vanua Levu, where Savusavu is located, is to the north and Viti Levu, where Suva and Nadi and the airport are located, is to the south. There are about three-hundred smaller islands scattered around. The east side of the island groups are lush jungle and very rainy (Suva is on the east side). The west side, which is my favorite, is dry and sunny. The west side is where most of the tourist resorts are located, as is Nadi and the main airport. There are so many places and islands to visit that a yacht could spend years cruising Fiji.

Most yachts sail south to Viti Levu to Suva and some of the more popular islands, and then on to the Yasawa Group. We decided to sail a route less traveled and went east and then north over the top of Vanua Levu visiting the most remote parts of Fiji where sometimes we were the only yacht the village had seen in years. Steve loved every minute of it. For me it was lonely at times, as I missed the other cruisers and went weeks without seeing a market. We lived off the land and sea as the villagers do. We sailed this route for a couple different reasons. We have cruising friends from three years ago in Mexico who sailed to Fiji and have never left. They sailed to a very remote village, fixed some things for the villagers, and the chief gave them their own beautiful seventy-five acre island.

We had books from New Zealand for their village school and wanted

190

to see their island. Also, by traveling this route, we could end up in the northern part of the Yasawa group and work our way down. There is so much to tell, it could fill another book. Here's the nutshell version.

We left Savusavu and headed East with daily stops along the way in beautiful bays. One of the lovely bays we visited was Viani Bay. After sailing all night we arrived to anchor in clear water off the village. It was Sunday morning and the drums were beating for church service. Then the singing began. The voices of a pureness I have never heard in my life. When we went to shore to meet the people we were treated like family and brought fruit and lemonade and invited to dinner. We stayed for three days and visited the school, swam and snorkeled and helped net fish off the reef. I was presented a beautiful tapa cloth (traditional art made from the bark of a tree and painted). I will treasure it always.

Listin, the young minister from the church, was attending a conference in a bay, which we would be sailing past on our way north, so we said we would take him with us. The next day, when we were getting ready to leave, Listin brought papayas, bananas, coconuts and a friend (in true Fijian fashion). Whenever you invite a Fijian or two to your boat, just double the number. They never come alone. So we had Listin and Kelly. Kelly happened to be an old fishing boat captain and knew shortcuts through the reefs to the bay. Kelly began to direct Steve through the reefs but finally Steve just turned the tiller over to Kelly and let him steer us through ten miles of shallow uncharted water. He knew these waters so well from canoe fishing there all of his life, we felt safer with him at the helm and he was beaming at the opportunity to pilot such a fine yacht. We had an interesting sail through areas we would never have sailed, since we didn't know these waters. We finally arrived where Kelly and Listin were attending their conference, said our goodbyes and we continued onto Rabi island.

Rabi Island is another beautiful island, only its inhabitants are from Ocean Island (Gilbert Islanders) and look more Polynesian than

Fijian. They have straight hair instead of the kinky hair of the Fijian. Seems the British strip-mined their island till it was uninhabitable and then transplanted them to Rabi Island. They are not as friendly as Fijians, but nonetheless friendly. We were visited by several outrigger canoes and given fruit. We made a couple other overnight stops on the way to Also Island where our friends Jim and Kyoko on sailing vessel *Also Two,* now live.

This was a nice place to visit but I wouldn't want to live here. The island that the chief gave to Jim and Kyoko is large (about one mile long) and densely wooded with two small sand beaches. It is about two miles from the village. They have done much clearing and have built a boat shed and several other outbuildings and a nice deck. Someday they will build a house. Kyoko has planted many fruit trees and a garden.

Jim and Kyoko love it here and Steve said he could live here, however I could never take the isolation. Even though the local village is two miles away, you have to wait for high tide to take a boat there as it's on another island. The village is small and there are only a few supplies at the local store. The people are lovely, but I can only take so much basket weaving and broom making. I just need more mental stimulation and like-minded people to talk with.

After about a week at anchor at Also Island, I started to feel the sting of loneliness. I was alone on the boat one day as Steve was helping Jim in the boat shed and having a great time and Kyoko, who is a loner, was off fishing in her boat. I am a people person and not a loner. Loners do better cruising on sailboats. I can only read so much in a day or cook a bit and then I need to talk with someone—anyone.

Alone on the boat at anchor I began to cry. I had this hole inside of me, this emptiness I couldn't seem to fill. It's called loneliness and I don't do well with it. The boat is rocking and trying to comfort me but all I can do is cry. I want to call a friend, but there is no phone. I want to jump on my bike or get in my car and ride into town, but there is no town and no bike or car. I cry some more. When will I see like-minded people again; friends, community, activities? I want to go home, wherever that might be. I want girl-friends and I want neighbors. I want to be involved in activities. I want a house and a dog and a garden. This for me is the most difficult part of cruising.

Damn Steve anyway. He's more of a loner than I am. This loneliness doesn't seem to bother him. But if he happens to return to the boat (and he has) when I'm in this space, he quickly learned that Sharon needs people. It's good to learn who you are and what your needs are, but out at sea, alone on a boat, is a difficult learning curve. Eventually I see someone on shore; I wave and decide to swim in and make a new friend. My tears get wiped away with the ocean. I will survive.

The day after we arrived at Also Island was a Sunday and we attended the village church and had to sit up front with the preacher since we were honored guests. I got into trouble for making faces and waving to the kids.

They also had a huge dinner in our honor. The men and "guest," meaning me, eat first, then children (boys first) and last women. I tried to help the women with the American way of ladies first, and they loved the idea but old ways are hard to change. Steve thought the idea of men eating first was great. We were the first visitors in over a year and we were the main attraction for the week. We visited the school and delivered books and I read from my poetry book. I spent a day helping with the kindergarten class and another day learning to make a Fijian broom with the ladies (this is one of my prized treasures) and another day washing clothes in the river.

Steve repaired two generators and word got around to the village across the bay, so they came to ask if Steve could fix theirs. We both went as I wasn't going to be left behind. Steve once again fixed another generator. We were asked to attend a party on Saturday night. When I asked whom the party was for, I was told the teacher's husband. When I asked if it was his birthday they informed me he had died and this was the one-hundred day wake. What a party! A wake is a bigger event than a wedding. People came from every village around bringing more food than I have ever seen. Seating is always cross-legged on the floor. There was pork, beef, turtle, chicken, salads and veggies. The list goes on and on. There were balloons, flowers, decorations and kava drinking and dancing. It's too bad the guest of honor couldn't be there. I danced with one of the single male teachers and the children just howled with delight. They have this ridiculous rule that a Fijian can't dance with anyone from the same village, so they get all excited when a visitor arrives that likes to dance. Boy do they dance sexy! I didn't want to stay here too long as I was afraid the chief may want to give Steve an island and we could be stuck here forever. I was beginning to miss civilization.

After leaving Also Island we did a two-day passage in twenty-five knot winds on the nose to a very remote island in Fiji. If you look at a map, you may see the island in the middle on the very northern top of Vanua Levu. It was so difficult to get there that I wasn't sure we should go, but it turned out to be another experience of a lifetime. When we arrived at this most lush green island with white sand beaches and the most beautiful blue water I have ever seen, we were greeted by three fishermen from the village who immediately led us around the island to a mooring off a beautiful private beach. I found out later, there is no such thing as privacy when near a Fijian village. Within an hour, three more fishing boats arrived and we had twelve Fijian fishermen on the boat. Their village was around the corner and would we please join them later for dinner. I had to decline as I needed to rest and I politely asked them to leave. Later that night while eating our dinner two more small local boats had arrived and I had to tell them we needed to sleep. We now had met half the men in the village.

The next day we saw several young girls sitting on the beach. They had been waiting for hours to greet us as we rowed to shore. They led the way via a path to the village so we could present our kava to the chief. When visiting a Fijian village, a woman must always wear a sulu. Men can wear shorts. It's a man's world here and I have difficulty with that. These women even wear a sulu swimming, although I gave some of the young women swimsuits and they loved them. It didn't take long before we were invited to have dinner with the family of Osea, brother-in-law of the chief and an old village elder (sixty-four years old). Then they found out Steve had fixed a few generators and they had him look at old the village generator, which was not working (surprise!). While I visited with the ladies, Steve worked till dark, with a dozen village men holding lanterns and looking on. Then there was the roar of an engine and the lights came on! The entire village, some two-hundred people, cheered and clapped. The chief came out and started dancing. They hadn't had lights in over two years. Steve was a hero!

The next day, when we came into the village, they presented us with flowered lei's around our neck and had a feast with kava drinking and dancing. The entire village declared a holiday. We had brought light to their village. I danced with every man in the village, including the chief. On this island, we were given a rare gift of the golden cowrie shell. My old shell book says it is one of the more rare shells and worth several hundred dollars, maybe more.

I overheard the ladies on this island talking about one of the local boys who had traveled to the mainland and learned to be a massage therapist. They said he gave wonderful massages. I quickly asked where I could locate him as I could sure use a massage. They soon introduced me to the tall, dark, muscular, good looking young man. When I asked him if I could get a massage, he said, "Yes, follow me." I didn't expect one that soon but I followed him to the chief's home. I was a bit puzzled but soon found out that in Fiji, a woman, especially a married one, cannot be alone with a single man. So the chief's wife sat in her chair to observe this massage. In Fiji your legs must be covered at all times, even during a massage, so I left my sulu on. However, taking your top off is perfectly okay, so I was asked to remove my top. It was a bit embarrassing but the massage was the best I have ever had; I soon forgot to be embarrassed. And the chief's wife approved it. Total cost $5F.

Steve

The villager's had been talking about this cannon on top of the mountain. I thought maybe a World War II relic. So I asked if I could go up to see it and they said sure, just a twenty-minute hike. Surely they must have a good trail to this site. Our friend Osea volunteered to show me the way, although he had only been there once before in his life. First, we hiked to the next village where we picked up Osea's young nephew to act as our guide. Then we began our assent to the mountain. It's not that high, maybe a thousand feet but it took an hour and a half to get up there, climbing almost straight up through brush, grass and rock (no trail at all). Finally at the summit we found just a flat area covered in tall grass. The nephew began hacking away at the tall grass with his machete and there it was—an old black powder cannon in beautiful condition. It must have been off an old sailing ship maybe two-hundred years old. But nobody knows or can remember how it got up there. It's a big one. I would guess it weighs four or five hundred pounds. I can't imagine how they got that thing up the mountain; it was all I could do to get up there myself. Anyway, they said I was the first *white man* ever to see it and most of the people on the island have never been up there. I took a lot of pictures so the rest of the folks in the village could see it. I did get some stunning photos with our boat anchored in the clear blue lagoon below. When I get a chance someday, l will do some research on the cannon and see if we can figure out how old it is and where it came from. Meanwhile, they gave me the hero's treatment again for having the courage to scale the mountain to see this cannon that is some kind of mysterious legend to most of the villagers.

Sharon

While Steve was hiking to the cannon, I had Rosy, Osea's daughter, out to the boat for lunch. I was not welcome on the hike because I was a woman and women are second-class citizens in much of Fiji. Rosy reinforced that for me as she told me her story.

196

Rosy is a beautiful thirty year old that has three sons. She had a boyfriend and was pregnant with her third son, when her father came to get her. Seems Osea did not like the boyfriend and wanted Rosy to leave and she refused. Osea then beat his daughter and took her home where he thought she belonged. Rosy has been home for two years helping her father with the local store they run but wants to leave. She told me that as soon as she gets a chance, she will leave and go to live with her sister in Suva. She said her father beats her often and she is tired of it. She wants a better life for herself and her sons.

While she was visiting on our boat, we made a healthy lunch and I gave her a swim suit that she looked beautiful in. I was concerned as I know in Fiji, women cannot wear a swimsuit, but she was so excited to have one. She said she would go to a private beach and wear it. I hope Osea never finds out.

We could write so much more about our two weeks on this remote island . I wish you could have been there to see the feast and the dancing. I would like to tell you about the time they took us in the village boat to Labasa (an all day trip) to do some shopping, or the times I walked across the island with the ladies to take lunches to the school kids, or the night the children did their Meke dance for us. I would like to tell you about the beautiful singing in church, or the time the ladies had a costume contest and they dressed me in a Fijian wedding dress, but it would fill another book.

The night before we left, the village children and my dear friend Rosy walked us to the beach with lanterns and sang their Fijian farewell song as we rowed back to our boat. It was very dark that night so no one could see the tears running down our cheeks. This island will always be my Fijian Island home.

Listen

Sharon Reed-Hendricks

Listen and you will hear
The song of every bird
In the quiet you will hear
The sounds you never heard

Look and you will see
Among the thorns - a rose
You'll find what you are looking for
Your eyes will never close

Breathe and you will smell
The scent of earth and sea
Breathe so deeply from within
The breath of what you'll be

Taste and you will know
The sweetness of the day
Sprinkle with a little spice
And savor it away

Touch and you will feel
So deeply you must cry
Touch the core within your being
And you will touch the sky

16   The Yasawa Islands

Sharon

Bula is one of the most used words in Fiji. It means hello, good morning, and good afternoon—just about anything you want it to mean. Steve has a couple of bula shirts (flowered Hawaiian type). There are bula cafés, bula clothes, and bula resorts. Bula is Fiji. Fiji is so beautiful, but it is a cruising sailor's navigation nightmare due to the numerous outlining reefs and very old charts of that area. We found the charts could be off from the GPS by up to a half a mile in some places. To get into any anchorage in Fiji, you must navigate your way between the reefs. There is usually a small opening through which you enter with crashing waves on either side. Someone must be watching at all times, usually from the bow.

They say there are two kinds of boats in Fiji: Those that have gone on the reef and those that are going to go on the reef. Several of our cruising buddies did hit reefs and one sailing boat from Denmark hit and sunk, the crew of three were missing for about a week. They were found in their life raft by an Australian warship between Tonga and Fiji. All three were alive and well, but the boat was a total loss. Well, anyway, we sailed Fiji without hitting a reef. We actually circumnavigated all of Fiji; including Vanua Levu and Viti Levu, the big islands, and many of the outlining islands. We saw so much of Fiji, from the remote villages to the bustling big cities and the beautiful, long, white-sand beaches and crystal clear waters of the outer islands. Needless to say, we loved Fiji.

We left the remote northern island (sometimes I was afraid of being left there) and headed for the Yasawa Islands. Steve's cannon story of being the first white man to hike to the cannon on top of the mountain is still being told amongst the cruising fleet.

Many shell collectors envy my treasured, rare golden cowry shell. The day Steve fixed the village generator and brought *light* to the remote

199

village for the first time in over two years and the chief declaring a holiday with feasting and dancing in our honor will be etched in our memory forever. They would have given us property to build a home but the village life is not the way I want to live forever. It sounds so *idyllic*, living on a beautiful tropical island, swimming and fishing all day, and joining in village activities. But in truth, I would get tired of this quickly and need more mental stimulation. Also it's not always as *idyllic* as it appears. There is a real pecking order to village life and there is no such thing as privacy. If someone is older, like a sister or cousin, they can take what they want from you at any time. For example; clothes, jewelry, a radio. There is no incentive to accumulate much wealth (unless of course you're old). Nonetheless, our visit to this remote island will always be a highlight of our trip to Fiji. From this island we did a two day sail "over the top" to the northernmost part of the Yasawa Islands.

On the northwest side of Viti Levu Island, looking like a string of blue beads lying on the horizon, are the beautiful South Pacific islands of the Yasawas—long stretches of sandy white beaches fringed by crystal clear, azure water. In one word, they are gorgeous and for the most part, undeveloped.

The Yasawa group is volcanic in origin; so many of the islands have lush, toweringly high mountains as a backdrop. This is truly a South Seas paradise. And the weather is dry and sunny. The group comprises six large islands and many smaller ones. There are a few isolated resorts and a scattering of backpackers' resorts, but other than that we had many anchorages to ourselves.

Since we sailed over the top of Vanua Levu from the remote island, we made landfall on the northernmost part of the island chain and worked our way south through the islands, visiting almost every island in the group and ending at Musket Cove, a resort and marina and a most popular place for cruising yachts to stop. Many cruisers sail direct to Musket Cove and stay there for the entire season, missing so much of the islands and villages of Fiji.

Yasawa Island

This northernmost island is the largest in the chain, and the one after which the chain was named. The island is about twenty-two kilometers long, and as we sailed along close to shore, I had never seen more isolated and beautiful stretches of white, sandy beaches. We just couldn't decide which beach to anchor off. I was all villaged-out by this time and could hardly wait to be alone and run naked on a beach. For almost six weeks we had been part of a village and had to wear a sulu everywhere, including swimming. So needless to say, I was so excited to see these deserted beaches with no villages. We stayed in this deserted anchorage five wonderful, relaxing, sunny days; swimming, snorkeling, eating lobster, collecting shells, watching beautiful sunsets, and, yes, running naked on the beach. I felt like a little girl again.

It was during our time on Yasawa that Steve and I had a serious discussion about where to go from here. Our money is disappearing quickly since we cannot live off our interest like we did before the stock market crash. We live very cheaply out here, but our funds are dwindling and we have only enough left for a year or two. We knew we would have to work out here somewhere, but where? I thought we were headed to Australia and could work there, but Steve wasn't so sure we could make enough money there and it would be much farther from home for a visit. We considered the Marshall Islands as they are U.S. Territory and one can work there, but again, a long ways away. We also thought about Japan, but it's a long hard sail and because of typhoon season it would take over a year just to get there. Steve thought of Hawaii since it's still in the tropics and easier to work in the United States. I was not happy about this idea at all. I knew from other cruisers that the trip to Hawaii (four-thousand miles) was a most difficult one against the wind, seas and current, and given the fact I hate passages anyway, this one did not sit well with me. We had some heated discussions about this one. All our cruising friends were headed to Australia and we had our charts and guidebooks and I was geared and excited about going that way. I didn't want to look at Steve's point of view. I was angry, sad and confused. I did not

want to make that passage! It was not a good time for the crew
of *Poet's Place*.

I did what I always do (after I cried and pouted). I networked.
To see just how awful it was, I sent emails to cruising friends
who went to Hawaii last season to work. They came back with
glowing reports about living and working in Hawaii. They
said as long as you could live on your boat (which they did)
it surprisingly wasn't as expensive as they thought it might be.
They said there were plenty of jobs and they could even help us
get one. They loved the weather, and the only problem was finding
space in a marina, but they managed and assured us we would
too. This did not make me happy, as I wanted to go the other
direction. They even said the passage wasn't too great but there
are several stops along the way, like Samoa, Cook Islands and the
Line Islands. Now I was really confused and just wanted to stay
in Fiji. So we put Hawaii on hold as an option while continuing
to cruise the Yasawas. As we sailed on, I was thinking Australia.
Steve was thinking Hawaii.

Sawa-i-lau
This tiny limestone island just off Yasawa Island is famous for
one thing; its underwater caves. Actually, there are many
caves all over the island.

As we entered the lovely bay off the island, I saw the first cruising
boat I had seen in over six weeks. I was so excited to see another cruising boat that I could hardly contain myself. As soon as we dropped
anchor I was on the VHF radio calling them. It was friends from
England on S/V *First Light*. We knew Christine and Richard, but not
very well. By the end of a month we knew them quite well as we
shared anchorages and dinners, hikes and swims. It helped to talk with
someone else about our dilemma of where to go from here. Christine
and Richard had been cruising for about ten years (twice as long as we
had) and it was helpful to get their input. Of course, they wanted us to
go on to Australia with them. I agreed. However Richard had lived in
Hawaii at one time and loved it.

One of the first things we did at Sawa-i-lau was to swim in the famous caves. Inside one large cave is a fresh water pool illuminated by the sun. You swim with a flashlight through a small orifice that connects the large cave to a smaller cave and pool. There are several of these caves that connect underwater. I entered one and Steve entered several. In the main cave are rock paintings of uncertain origin and antiquity. According to our Lonely Planet guidebook, one historian thought the inscriptions bore a resemblance to Chinese characters. We spent about a week here exploring above and below the water, and Christine and I did some shelling on the white-sand beaches.

Blue Lagoon (Turtle Island)
A half-day sail downwind (my kind of sailing) was the idyllic, lagoon where they filmed the movie Blue Lagoon, which is now the name of the area. You really need good light to weave your way through the reefs here. As we zigzagged through the reefs, I was mesmerized by the beauty and color of the water outlined by the white-sand beach and swaying palms. I was surprised there were no other yachts in the lagoon, so *First Light* and *Poet's Place* had the place to ourselves. Within three days there were six cruising yachts in the lagoon. We had potluck dinners on the beach, snorkeling on the reefs, hiking across the island and a great community of friends.

Every day a local farmer from a nearby island came out in his outrigger full of fresh produce to sell us. It was great to have delivery service and just pick out our produce from the comfort of our cockpit. This was my kind of place, but there were more islands to explore. After a week of this lovely anchorage we moved on to the next island in the group.

Naviti Island (Somosomo Village)
This was another lovely bay, but a bit uncomfortable due to choppy seas, so we only stayed a day. The village of Somosomo has the only woman chief in the Yasawas. We went ashore to the village to bring the customary kava to present to the chief. I am getting tired of these kava ceremonies and much prefer ice tea

in the cockpit.

This island has seen a lot more cruisers than some islands. A cruise ship also visits them once a month, so they are more tourist oriented. They tried to sell us jewelry and shells (things I was given at other islands) and I might add, my gifts from those islands were much nicer. I simply told them I had no money with me. It was obvious this was not a poor village. They seem to have everything they needed and much of what they wanted. Tourism has changed this village. The next day we moved around the corner to a calmer bay and did some exploring. We had read about a sunken World War II plane in the area and wanted to dive on it.

Steve
As the story goes, a Navy pilot was reported lost on a ferry flight (moving the plane from one base to another) of his Grumman Hellcat fighter during World War II. The Navy wrote it off as lost, but six months later the pilot's brother traveled to Fiji to search for his brother's remains, so that he might return them home for a proper funeral. His search led him to a small, remote village, where he found his brother alive and well, being well taken care of by a beautiful young Fijian woman. Reluctantly, he returned home with his brother. The plane was fine but he had just run out of fuel and landed it on the beach. But the next hurricane that came blew it into the lagoon, and there it has remained for the past sixty years. From where we anchored we rowed ashore, hiked across the island and dove into what is now known as Hellcat Lagoon. It was exciting to find remains of this old aircraft lying in about ten feet of water. The aluminum parts were intact and in surprisingly good condition.

Sharon
We also did some outstanding snorkeling on a reef just in front of where we were anchored. I had never seen anything like it. There were cliffs of multicolor, mushroom-type coral in every

shape and color, soft coral in pastels and fish the colors of which I have never seen; it was like being in an underwater garden. I hadn't seen anything like this since Tonga's Hapi group two years ago. I never tired of diving on these beautiful reefs. There are times I think I could live underwater.

Nan Uya

By this time *First Light* had sailed off in another direction and we were alone again, but not for long. As we pulled into the lovely bay of the next island, there were four boats already anchored there. One of the boats was from Brazil. We had not seen them since Tonga two years before. We had previously sailed with them from Panama and throughout the Pacific. It was so nice to catch up with them and learn the whereabouts of other cruisers.

There was a backpackers' resort on the beach and cruisers are always welcome at these places. Most welcome you for dinner or lunch for a fee of $5F, which is about $2.50US, cheaper than eating on the boat. But we never made it in for dinner, as that afternoon a storm hit us with sixty knot winds and a whiteout. Talk about scary! No one left their boat and two of the boats drug anchor and crashed into other boats. We experienced two such storms (mini-cyclones) while in Fiji this year, both of them while we were at anchor.

Drawaqa Island

After several days of waiting for a good weather window, we left to sail to Waya. We chose the wrong day to leave, (thirty knot head-winds) and couldn't make progress. I hated every minute of it and we decided to try a little tiny island halfway to Waya. This turned out to be a great anchorage out of the wind. The little island had a lovely sand beach and some cliffs in the background. The place looked deserted but I thought I heard a baby cry. When I looked around on the beach I saw some wild baby goats. I could hardly wait to get to shore and explore. Of course, the baby goats quickly returned to mama on the cliffs, and I continued hunting for shells. We swam in the crystal clear water, watched a sunset and were thankful for this little island refuge out of the storm.

Waya Island
We didn't stay long enough or visit all of the anchorages on this beautiful island. We were trying to make Musket Cove, as several friends whom we had not seen for some time were there and soon to be leaving. Waya is a big island with towering mountains of lush, green, beautiful beaches, and a scattering of small villages. It is lovely—actually breathtaking. I decided you could spend years just exploring the Yasawa Islands. The water is so clear, the diving superb and the weather is warm and sunny. It's too bad cyclone season chases all the yachts away.

Navadra Island
This is another beautiful island with three long, sandy beaches, more goats on shore, lots of shells and fantastic snorkeling on the reefs. It's hard to believe that these beautiful anchorages are so empty. Most of the cruising boats like the company of other boats so they hang out at Musket Cove.

Musket Cove
After an all-day motor-sail we arrived at the famous Musket Cove Resort and anchored amongst the fifty other yachts. Now I know why the Yasawa anchorages are empty. Musket Cove is a lovely resort and marina with clear, blue water and white-sand beaches. The resort has several bures (small houses) for tourists, several restaurants, a couple of small grocery stores with great local and New Zealand products. It has several swimming pools, a few boutiques and gift shops, an airport, bike/kayak/windsurf rentals and a nice mooring and anchorage area. They also boast a three dollar bar, which consists of a thatched roof bar, several covered tables and a huge barbeque pit where every night cruisers can gather and bring something to cook (the resort has the fire going), buy a drink (all drinks are $3F) and enjoy the company of friends. They welcome cruisers and we can use all of the facility as if we were hotel guest. We could swim in the pools, eat at the restaurants, hike the trails, swim the beaches and basically enjoy the resort like a tourist while living on your boat. For one dollar you can join the Musket Cove Yacht Club and become a

206

lifetime member, which entitles you to all the luxuries of the re-sort. We anchored, which was free, and stayed about two weeks enjoying the resort and visiting with other cruisers. Most cruising friends were getting ready to sail to Australia. Of course, they all wanted us to join them and I was ready. But we headed east (I fig-ured we could always turn around) against the wind, current, and seas and against my decision, and eventually to Hawaii to work.

Robinson Crusoe Island

Sailing east around the bottom of Viti Levu with headwinds of 30 knots, we decided to turn into a protected bay to get out of the weather and quiet the unhappy First Mate. After navigating through the reefs, we dropped the anchor in one of the most calm, clear, blue-green lagoons I have ever seen. There appeared to be a little island with a white-sand beach and a resort of some sort. As I was starting dinner a staff person from the island resort rowed out to our boat to invite us in for dinner and a Polynesian dancing show. The dinner would cost us $5F ($2.50US) and the show was free. The buffet all-you-can-eat dinner was great and the Polynesian dancing show was outstanding and included fire dancing.

As it turned out, this was an upscale backpackers' resort called Robinson Crusoe Island and what a place it was! Three Aus-tralian couples about our age live and work here, and love to visit with the cruising yachts. Most of the backpacking guests are in their twenties, so the Australians like having someone more their age to talk with. We were welcome to join them for dinner or lunch anytime for $5F. We could also watch the show any night, go snorkel-ing with the guests and join in the jewelry making, turtle viewing, coconut-tree climbing and basket weaving, all for free. This was my kind of place. I signed up for everything. We had another one of those mini-cyclones hit while we were at anchor here with sixty-five knot winds and whiteouts.

Steve

One stress of cruising life is the worry of how your anchor will hold in the next windstorm. I love watching the weather; it can be really exciting and sometimes too exciting. Here at Robinson Caruso we were anchored in fifteen feet of water on hard packed sand and felt pretty secure. Then we saw this big black squall coming our way. Fortunately we were on the boat and not on shore at that time or this story could have ended here. We quickly put down a second plow anchor and let out two-hundred-fifty feet of chain and tied down everything lose to brace for the storm. As the storm hit, the wind was screaming through the rigging. The anchor chains were stretched bar tight as the bow bucked up and down in the wind as we were being pushed towards the beach. Visibility was reduced to fifty feet by the driving rain but we could see one other boat move past, narrowly missing us as she dragged anchor. (Fortunately her anchor caught hold before she hit the beach). With the wind speed indicator showing gust to 65 knots, we started the engine in hopes the thrust from our little propeller would help hold us against the wind and keep the anchors from breaking lose. I had to stay out in the rain to try and steer to keep the bow pointed straight into the wind. I put on a dive mask to protect my eyes from the driving rain. Finally after twenty minutes of fighting to hold our position, the storm passed, leaving calm muddy water around us. On shore there was a lot of damage and seaweed swept out of the lagoon by the wind and was piled three feet deep on what earlier had been a perfect white sand beach. This experience is one more reason it will be nice to get back to a dock in Hawaii. Sharon missed her jewelry making class that day.

Sharon
One day Wayne, one of the owners of the resort, took us into town. First we went by high speed boat, driven by one of the Fijian staff, through the mangrove-lined river. Then we were taken by van into the charming little town of Singatoka. By this time, we were already checked out of Fiji with the officials and supposedly on our way to Samoa. We had only planned to stay out of the weather that one night. It was now day seven and we were having too much fun at Robinson Crusoe. It was about this time that I ran into some friendly police-men who invited me in to see their newly decorated station and wanted their picture taken. Here I was, illegal in the country, being

entertained by the police force of Singatoka. Steve was sure I would end up in jail.

Robinson Crusoe turned out to be one of Fiji's best-kept secrets. We stayed ten days and really enjoyed our visit. I was in no hurry since we were heading northeast to Hawaii, but there are many stops on the way. And what fun we are having. Maybe we'll never make it to Hawaii.

Next stop Samoa, and just in time for festival week.

From Where You Came

Sharon Reed-Hendricks

You can never go back from where you came
Expecting things to be the same
The way it was you will not find
Life moves forward - not behind

Things didn't stand still while you were gone
They change and grow and carry on
Sometimes you will not recognize
The place, the face, sometimes the size

The place and sometimes people too
Might differ from the ones you knew
The longer that you've been away
The more the change - It's hard to stay

If you must go - or move away
And then return - but not to stay
So much you knew won't be the same
It's now the place from where you came

17 Western Samoa, Fanning Island and Hawaii

Sharon

We missed this part of the Pacific on our way west, so it was marvelous to experience it even though the passage getting here was thirteen days of pure hell. We were both crashing and bashing into heavy winds and seas (remember, we're going the wrong way) or drifting as there was no wind at all. I do hate passages but in hindsight it's a small price to pay for a life-style of freedom, one that I fear I may be losing by heading back to the states.

We arrived (limped into) in Apia, Western Samoa with a torn headsail, a leak in the fresh water tank and an engine that didn't work because it had dirty fuel in the tank. We made all repairs in the month we spent in Samoa while enjoying the islands, the people and the culture. I must admit the weather in Samoa was hot, even for me, but I loved it. It doesn't cool down at night like many of the South Pacific islands. Western Samoa is very different than America Samoa. Although we did not go to American Samoa, we heard that most of the people in America Samoa are on the dole, so the harbor and main area are very depressed and dirty. This is another example of our government coming in and changing the culture. In Western Samoa, although very poor, it is very beautiful and villages, for the most part, were very neat and tidy with flowers everywhere. There was a sense of community and caring. We heard from other cruisers that American Samoa wasn't worth the stop because of the crime, filth and a harbor that was littered with debris, making anchoring unsafe.

The most unique characteristic of Samoa was the fale (home). A fale is an oval structure without walls as the weather is so hot you don't need them. Wooden poles support the thatched roof and the floor consists of a platform of coral

211

rock which kind of looks like a gazebo. The entire building is constructed without nails; the rafters and joints being tied with coconut fibers. Blinds are made of woven pandanus mats and are lowered to keep out wind and rain. There is not much privacy as the entire family sleeps in the same open area. There is often a small kitchen fale near the main home, usually in the back, used for meal preparation. Fales are usually sparsely furnished. They most often contain a clothes chest, sometimes several suitcases, and several sleeping and sitting mats. The more modern fales may contain tables and chairs, kitchen appliances, televisions and videos, however I didn't see many.

Every village has one prominently elevated fale talimalo in which the village council meets. The village women keep it clean and decorated. The village also has a committee who makes sure each fale is clean and that kitchen and toilets meet village health standards. The government of Western Samoa holds an annual competition and awards a prize to the village most cared for. Wouldn't that be a great idea for America Samoa.

Western dress is becoming more the norm with the younger people, but the lava lava, a wraparound unisex piece of brightly colored material, worn throughout the pacific islands, is still worn by most. I, myself, prefer the lava lava (sulu or sarong) as they are comfortable and cool. I even got Steve to wear one once or twice. They also wear them in Hawaii. Most Samoans speak English, but the common language is Samoan. I was able to pick up a few words while I was there.

Apia is the capital of Western Samoa, and we anchored *Poet's Place* in the harbor right off of the town. There has been much British and New Zealand influence in Apia since WW II and it is apparent in the capital city. One of the landmarks is the clock tower in the town center. It was built in memory of those Western Samoans who were killed in WW II. Along the waterfront peninsula there are several British and American Memorials along with a

German monument. There is also the famous Aggie Grey Hotel. Every weekday morning at 7:50 a.m. the police band marches up Beach Road to the courthouse for the flag raising ceremony at 8:00 a.m. The traffic is stopped for the show and we could hear them from our boat as they played their foot-tapping march. The men and women in the band wore uniforms of light blue skirts, sandals, blue police jackets and white pith helmets; very unique. One morning we ate breakfast at the Sails Restaurant upstairs balcony, where Robert Louis Stevenson often dined and watched this colorful parade.

In 1889 the already famous Scottish author and poet, Robert Louis Stevenson arrived in Apia. He left Europe for relief from the tuberculosis he was suffering from and fell in love with Western Samoa. He purchased a piece of property and built a home in the hills above Apia. He named it Vailima. His health improved some but his time there was a short four years. He loved the Samoan people and they loved him. They named him Tusitala, which means teller of tales. It was there at *Vailima* he wrote his famous poem that ends with the lines, "Home is the sailor, home from the sea. And the hunter home from the hill." He is one of my many admired writers and we visited and toured his home at *Vailima* with another cruising couple from England. We then hiked the hill to his grave, which was no easy feat but we were rewarded with a spectacular view of Apia and the water below. We rented a car with our cruising friends Neil and Greta from England and really got to see village life as we toured the entire island for three days.

We were so fortunate to be in Samoa during their annual culture festival. What a treat. The festival has contests, tournaments and events that last an entire week. Every evening on the grassy lawn in front of the government buildings we would spread our mats and settle ourselves with the rest of the cruisers and locals to watch the show for that night. Sunday was church choir competition, dance competition on Monday, Tuesday singing competition, Wednesday fire dancing; every night was better

213

than the next. During the day they had outrigger canoe races and long boat races. There was a floral parade with floats done in the most beautiful flowers. Saturday they had the Miss Samoa beauty contest. They came from America Samoa and all the outer islands to compete in this festival of events.

Steve

The long boats are unique sixty foot rowing boats manned by forty men rowing, one drummer beating cadence in the bow and a captain on the tiller shouting orders to his crew. This is truly a spectacular race to watch. We got to watch them practice right next to our boat every morning and every evening. The week climaxed with the final long boat races. The winning team were treated like national hero's honored in the parade the next day.

Sharon

The best of all the events, and the one I enjoyed the most, was held on Friday evening at the best hotel in Western Samoa. It was the *Miss Tooty Fruity* drag queen beauty pageant. What a hoot! I never laughed so much in my entire life. It was better than any beauty pageant I'd ever seen. This event has been held for six seasons now and is attended by all the high officials and wealthy citizens of Samoa. The cost was twenty dollars Samoan ($7US). This was expensive by Samoan standards, but worth every cent. The he/she's were lovely and at times we couldn't tell in the audience who was a he and who was a she. The pageant was almost three hours long and was even televised. They had the usual competition plus a few extras. They had the talent competition, the evening gown competition and the question time. They also had the undergarment competition where the he/she looked better than most women I know. There was also the favorite fruit competition, where the contestant dressed up as their favorite fruit. We had Miss Banana, with bananas dangling from everywhere, Miss Grape, with a giant grape for her/his body and one on the head, Miss Pineapple and Miss Cherry. You get the picture. When Miss Grape was walking down the aisle in the evening gown event she/he was draped in lovely jewelry. Upon close inspection I realized it looked like Catholic rosary beads. Sure enough it was and seated behind us was a row of Catholic nuns from the local orphanage just howling in laughter. The proceeds from the event went to the orphanage, which I thought was great. What an evening. It's one of the biggest and best-attended events of the festival. You see, in Samoa and many other South Pacific island groups, he/she's are a part of the culture and very respected.

By traditional definition, a fa'afafine is a male child brought up as a female due to a shortage of helping hands around the house. The word translated means simply "like a woman," but one senses that there is more to the custom than that. They dress as females, play female roles and get away with prom-iscuity that is forbidden to biological females. The neat part is there is no social stigma attached to their open flaunting of sexual preferences. Some do revert back to the male role upon reaching adulthood.

We spent almost two months in Samoa and loved every day. We really didn't want to leave, but once again the weather deter-mines a sailor's destination and Samoa is in the hurricane belt. We wanted to take our time enjoying all our stops along the way to a safe harbor (Hawaii?) so it was time to leave this beautiful country and once again head into the wind and seas.

Poet's Place and three other boats were headed to the Cook Is-lands but due to strong wind and seas on the nose, and the fact that we sail, not motor, it would have taken us months, so we decided to skip the Cooks. We had been to the Cooks on our way across the pacific heading west a few years before, so I wasn't too disappointed to get this passage over and make landfall somewhere else. One of the other boats which was a big one, actually made it but he motored a lot to get there. The rest of us headed to the Kiribati Islands of Christmas, or in our case, Fanning Island.

215

3 3 3

It was another long difficult passage against the winds and seas but not as bad as heading to the Cooks. We thought we might make it to Christmas Island but our heading was more in favor of Fanning. It took twenty one days from Samoa to Fanning. After hearing reports from other yachts that landed at Christmas, I'm glad we made landfall at Fanning as it is beautiful.

Fanning Island is part of the Line Island group that belongs to the Republic of Kiribati (pronounced Kari-bass). It is actually an atoll which means it is a lagoon encircled by a reef. The island consists of a series of islets with a beautiful lagoon in the middle. The Tuamotu Islands of French Polynesia are atolls. From the air an atoll looks like sparkling beads of a necklace. It is difficult to sail into an atoll as you must enter through a narrow pass between the reefs. This was very scary. Many boats hit the reefs if they are not careful and some are lost this way. We always enter during daylight hours and when it's slack or incoming tide, with one person on the bow as lookout while the other is steering the boat. Once inside it is calm and beautiful and looks like a picture postcard. The Republic of Kiribati is made up of the Gilbert Islands, Phoenix Islands and the Line Islands. It is very remote except for the fact that now Norwegian Cruise Line ships out of Hawaii stop there once a month. They get around the rule that a foreign flagged vessel cruising in U.S. (Hawaii) waters has to leave the country every month to avoid heavy taxes. So they offer a cruise around the islands of Hawaii along with an offshore stop in Fanning. It takes the cruise ship three days to sail the passage from Fanning to Honolulu and it took us twelve days. This has changed the flavor of the island somewhat, as the people now have some money from selling their crafts to the tourist on cruise ship day. It's quite an event to behold. The cruise ship anchors outside the reef and ferries the tourists to the island via water taxis. The cruise line leases property on the island from the government of Kiribati. There they have buildings for the cruise line use and even a caretaker named Roland. They also have water toys, sailing cats, bicycles and more for the four hour lunch stay at Fanning. I don't know how you get to see an island in four hours but that's what they do. I'm sure glad we cruise a different way. Four months isn't enough time, let alone four hours. During the month we were there we got to experience "cruise ship" day and since we look more or less like the tourists we just joined in for the lunch. There were three of us couples, from boats that were there at that time. They set up on the beach and have a nice spread. By this time I was running low on green veggies and it was nice to have my fill of salad. They even had veggie burgers. The three yachts anchored inside Fanning lagoon made quick friends with the Canadian caretaker, Roland, of the Norwegian Cruise Line. We were welcomed to use their facility and the bicycles to ride around the island anytime we wanted. This was great fun and since there are very few motorized vehicles (maybe two trucks and a few motorcycles) we really got to see the island.

We borrowed the bicycles several times, but one lovely hot sunny day six of us cruisers decided to take an all day tour around the entire island, about twenty miles total. Now I love to bike and I love to hike but this particular day we hiked with the bike. We were told before we ventured out, that to bike around the entire island was possible. However we would have to cross a couple of streams and carry the bikes across. This didn't sound too bad, as I pictured a shallow narrow stream like the one I saw on a previous bike ride. Well, let me tell you crossing the Amazon might have been easier. Some of the streams were chest deep for me and "a couple" does not mean two. I, along with Steve, stopped counting after crossing twelve streams and decided to stop and eat my lunch while the others who were all ten years younger I might add, continued on. I informed my *masochist* biker friends that I enjoy biking and I enjoy hiking but not hiking with a bike carried over my head. All in all it was a fun adventure and one I shall never forget, nor repeat.

We had so much fun and every day was a new adventure. Several times we hopped in our friends dinghy and motored out of the pass (the small entrance through the reefs) and waited for the tide change

217

when the water came rushing into the pass. We would then drift/ dive with snorkel gear through the pass. One person would hold on to the dinghy painter rope so we wouldn't lose the dinghy and we would just enjoy the underwater view while the tide would carry us through the pass at about 5 knots. What a sensation! We would see turtles, giant manta rays and sharks, hundreds of barracudas and an assortment of colorful fish. All the time we would be carried by the current through the pass like being on an underwater moving escalator. We did this several times a week during incoming tide.

One evening, when we were at Fanning Island, we were invited to a church fundraiser. We were honored guests so they made lei's for our necks and we sat on the front row mats with the officials and the men, The event hosted traditional dancing and singing along with a feast of food. The menu consisted of rice, taro in assorted forms, pork, chicken, dog meat, bananas, more rice, fish cooked in assorted ways, more rice and breadfruit. Times like this I'm glad to be a vegetarian. It was a beautiful night to behold.

Steve

Like most foreign countries we have visited, there is always a local ex-patriot that resides and rules his own little domain. He is usually married to a much younger local girl, which gives him the best of both worlds. These characters are a wealth of information and entertainment and there is usually one or more in each foreign village or town. Fanning island's ex-pat is Chuck and he lives with his island wife and her four sisters on his large, but not large enough, sailboat. Chuck has lived on Fanning for about six years now and knows anything and everything you want or don't want to know. Chuck and Roland, the cruise line caretaker, do not get along so we alternated days with them, as we liked spending time with both. Chuck owned a nice size sixteen foot skiff that held all his family and their friends. He invited two of us cruising couples to spend the day across the lagoon on another island to catch land crabs and have a feast. That's eighteen people in a sixteen foot boat.

218

Chuck picked us all up at our boats and ferried us over to the island on a lovely day. Every day is sunny and lovely on Fanning. Since the boat was slightly over loaded we towed two of the kids along behind on a surfboard.

As we hit the beach on this lovely part of the island the kids scattered and started grabbing crabs. The crabs were everywhere, hundreds of them. These are most interesting creatures as they have one very large claw and if you break it off they will grow another one. So while Chuck's wife was building a fire, everyone else was busy gathering a bushel full of crab claws for lunch. We steamed them over the fire and proceeded to eat crab legs till we couldn't move, then we took a nap.

Sharon
The island grows very little in the way of fruits and veggies. They have bananas and papaya, taro and some sweet potato but no lettuce, tomatoes, carrots and not a one onion or garlic. Thank goodness I carry plenty. They didn't even know what an apple or orange was. They exist on fish, rice, taro, and bananas. I could never live there as I need my fruits and veggies. This place is not in the hurricane belt so it's safe to stay here through the season, and some boats do, but I would starve—so Hawaii was looking better all the time.

We were looking at another not so fun passage. There were about eight sailing yachts heading to Hawaii from various places and it was nice to commiserate with them on the radio. After twelve long days against the wind, we arrived in a downpour and couldn't even see the island. Everyone said it hadn't rained like that in months and it was our fault since we are from Seattle. When we pulled into our slip at the yacht club in Honolulu, our long time cruising friends, Gene and Sherry graced our necks with lei's of flowers and welcomed us as we dripped in rainwater. The first thing I did was to take a long hot shower and have a big green salad. I have arrived at my new home—Hawaii.

Epilog—

Writing this book has been one of the most difficult and emotional pieces I have ever had to write. Writing about these countries and islands brought back memories and touched feelings about the cruising lifestyle that were heart wrenching. It was like writing about an old friend who has passed away and you know you will never see them again. It's something I want to avoid but cannot. Writing about it brings up the sadness I have been trying to deal with these past months while trying to adjust to the culture shock of the United States. The hi-rise buildings, the traffic, the prices, insurance and stress of living here are more than I can balance. After six years of the slow paced, healthy and inexpensive lifestyle I was living, I found I was having a difficult time fitting in. I was introduced to a different way of living and I embraced it with my soul. Now I feel like an alien in my own country. Steve seems to melt into the work world and the politics and stress seem to roll off him. I, on the other hand, felt empty and sad. There is another world out there where we don't have to play the game. I wonder sometimes how this country can call itself advanced and great when most of its population is over worked, over fed, over stressed and over taxed and not in touch with their feelings. The insurance and pharmaceutical companies have control of your health instead of you. And the government has control of your life. Only when you're away from it do you get to see what a hold they have on you. There is nothing I can do about the fact that I am here, but by having an attitude adjustment I have been able to go forward. As long as I have to be here, I might as well enjoy it and since I have to work to replenish our money, I might as well do it in style. I thought I would change my attitude when things got better. But actually it works the opposite. I had to first change my attitude, then things did get better.

Steve got a great job he likes as a facilities director at a university and I got into property management, which I find I really like. I always wanted a house on the beach someday so I am now managing a condo on the beach away from the noise of downtown Honolulu. The boat is at a marina nearby waiting for our weekend sailing excursions. What are the plans for the next adventure? I really don't know.

2012 Seven Years Later In Hawaii
Since we have been in Hawaii, we have had to deal with job losses, walking away from a condo I loved, Steve leaving the relationship but coming back and us living back on *Poet's Place*, the boat that I love.

When Steve left we both took a good hard look at our life and the relationship. We made a decision that we both wanted this relationship and we would do whatever it took to put it back together. We took the same attitude we had when we both decided to sail the world. It looked like we had very little, but we had a lot. We had each other and together we shared a dream. We worked hard at it and we never stopped focusing on that dream. And we did it—we sailed half way around the world. Because we work on the relationship we now have a better relationship than ever. When two people work together things happen twice as fast.

So here we are in Hawaii on *Poet's Place,* deciding what our next adventure will be and whether or not we want to sell the boat. That boat is so much of my life that I can't imagine selling her.

Sometimes *Poet's Place* rocks me to sleep at night and we talk about the days of sailing when we both were younger and happy just to be free and feel the wind. We cried together, we laughed together and to me she was real and alive. If that boat could talk—the stories she would tell.

Living the "normal life" is reality—Cruising was the dream.
Am I sorry we took the journey? No, not at all. I wouldn't have missed it for the world!

221

Sail Away

Sharon Reed-Hendricks

You ask me why I sail away
And what it's really worth
Why give up all the things you have
To sail around this earth

I go sailing for the freedom
And adventure that I find
I have room to live the fullest
For I left the stress behind

It's there I learn about my life
And why I need to wander
At sea I have the needed space
To question and to ponder

I can visit any country
And the cultures that I taste
Are the memories I'll savor
For a life that's slower pace

You say I don't have much
But less is really more
It's full of life's experience
Who could want for any more

And when my life is over
Looking back upon its worth
I'll discover that I really lived
Having sailed upon this earth

ABOUT THE AUTHORS

Sharon Reed-Hendricks is a poet, a writer and a business owner. She is also the author of the poetry books *Sharon Shares Her Heart* and *From Where Eagles Soar*. She lives in Ko Olina, Hawaii with her husband and best friend Steve.

Steve Hendricks is retired Director of Facilities at Hawaii Pacific University. He lives with his soul-mate Sharon on their sailboat *Poet's Place.*

For slide show presentations, book signings and other media inquiries—
visit: poetsplacesailing.com

Made in the USA
Monee, IL
06 December 2021

84080556R00134